PHOTOGUIDE
to
Colour Printing
from
Negatives and Slides

THE ⓟ PHOTOGUIDES

The
PHOTOGUIDE
to
Colour Printing
from
Negatives and Slides

Jack H. Coote
FRPS

Focal Press
London & New York

ISBN 0 240 50926 9

First edition 1976
Second impression 1977

Text set in 10/12 pt. Photon Univers, printed by photolithography and bound in Great Britain at The Pitman Press, Bath

Contents

There is a magic about colour printing that is irresistible. When you make a print in colour you are really conducting a kind of conjuring trick – a much more impressive one than when you make a print in black and white.

Until quite recently the steps required by any colour process were complex and lengthy, so that only a few amateurs could manage their own colour printing. But now, improvements in materials and equipment have made it almost as easy to make prints in colour as in black and white. Almost, but not quite, because although it is a simple matter to make a colour print of a kind, it is rather more difficult to make prints that really look right.

In a way, colour printing is a bit like painting – the next attempt is bound to produce the best picture we have ever made.

This book is arranged in the belief that once you have decided to try colour printing you will be impatient to get started. Only when you have met specific difficulties will you be inclined to read about their possible causes. From the second chapter you will be able to learn what you require and the simplest procedure to follow; then if you wish, you can dive straight in to make your first colour print. This first print – which you should keep as a memento – will certainly prove thrilling, but you *may* be forced to admit that it is not as successful as it could be.

At this point you may be ready to learn about some of the niceties of colour printing, and these things are dealt with in the remaining chapters of the book.

The Fascination of Making Colour Prints

Ever since the earliest days of photography when all colour prints had to be made by assembling three separate images in registered superimposition, colour printing has held a fascination that has captured the imagination of an ever increasing number of photographers. In the last few years colour printing processes have become much easier and this has meant that even the amateur can enjoy the excitement of making his own colour prints with quite modest equipment and facilities.

Not only have the processes and methods become simpler, the time required to make colour prints has been reduced dramatically. Not so long ago, you were lucky if you could get a good result after two evenings of work – the first evening was spent making a set of separation bromide prints or a set of dye-transfer matrices and the next evening you put the necessary three colour images together to see the result. Now, while you may have to spend a part of your first evening getting a balanced result with your particular enlarger and batch of paper, once this has been done you can expect to get several good prints during each session.

I have often wondered just why it is so fascinating to make a colour print, but I suppose any form of photography is miraculous – even the development of a black and white print in a dish – and if this is so, then to produce a colour print is so much more wonderful.

Until you have opened a print drum at the end of a processing sequence and removed your colour print, you can have no idea of the thrill it will give – particularly when you have got it right.

The creative element

Some enthusiastic amateur photographers – the Americans call them hobbyists – take the view that black and white printing allows more opportunity for self-expression than colour printing, but this is only true so long as perfectly straight prints are made from the original negative or slide. Once you have gained some confidence with a colour printing process it will not be long before you decide to modify your prints to suit your ideas. It is a relatively simple matter to darken skies or lighten shadow areas in order to reveal more detail. It is a bit more difficult to modify local areas of colour, but even this is well within your bounds as your skill and confidence increase. The very least you can do is to choose the degree of enlargement and the composition or cropping of the picture that you prefer — factors which are all decided for you when you order prints through your dealer.

Merits of negative/positive and positive/positive printing

At this point it might be as well to consider the relative merits of working via colour negatives or colour slides. I believe that some people are puzzled by the fact that there are these two ways of getting a colour print. Some amateurs have never used any colour film other than colour negative — simply having graduated from black and white negatives to colour negatives. They know that there is no problem in getting their exposed films processed and printed because the procedure, as far as the chemist or photo dealer is concerned, is exactly the same as it is for black and white films. Some amateurs use the occasional colour transparency film, but they are unlikely to use it when they really want prints. Most 'keen' amateurs have projectors and screens and use them regularly to display the slides they get from reversal colour films. This group, although usually very enthusiastic and well equipped, frequently seem to be under the impression that prints cannot be obtained from transparencies, or if they are then their quality is invariably disappointing.

There are several reasons why these impressions have been created, but the fact is that colour prints can be obtained from colour negatives and from colour transparencies.

Photofinisher prints

It is probably true that photofinishers, whose job it is to make the prints ordered by amateurs through chemists and dealers shops, do produce better prints from negatives than from transparencies. The reasons for this are a little complicated.

The two most important factors in the colour negative system are that the camera film has almost as much exposure latitude as a black and white film; and the characteristics of the negative image can be designed for the sole purpose of producing the best possible prints on paper. In other words the colour negative is a means to an end, unlike a transparency which is itself a finished photograph.

A correctly exposed and processed transparency has a much higher contrast than a negative of the same subject. This makes it more difficult to print from and sometimes either highlight or shadow details are lost. In addition, photographic manufacturers have found difficulty in making some colours come out well in colour reversal papers.

Having said all this it remains a fact that there are several reasons why the amateur who intends to start colour printing for the first time, should seriously consider the advantages of working from transparencies rather than negatives.

Advantages of printing from transparencies

The most important advantage that comes with printing from transparencies is that you can easily tell what the original photograph looks like, so you know if it has been properly exposed and if it is correct in colour balance. It is much more difficult to predict the kind of colour print that will result from any given colour negative, because both brightness and colour values are in reverse. Although a disadvantage in one respect, some advantage comes from the fact that the contrast of the colour transparency is relatively high, because then the contrast of the reversal printing paper must necessarily be relatively low. This means that enlarging exposure times are not so critical neither is colour filter adjustment so sensitive.

Integrated printing of colour negatives

If you are wondering why it is that colour negative printing presents problems to amateurs which do not worry the photofinisher, it is because the finisher will be using automatic integrating printers costing £10,000 or more. These machines are capable of looking at a negative photo-electrically and very rapidly assessing the correct printing exposure and colour balance. Working in this automatic way can result in first time balanced prints from some 95% of all negatives.

So you see, you have a choice to make and only you can make it. Much will depend on which of the two types of colour film you normally use, because the best thing is to start by printing from some of your favourite negatives or transparencies to see how you get on.

Having used both colour negative and colour transparency films at different times I must admit that the wide exposure latitude of colour negative materials always gives me a comfortable feeling because I know that provided my exposures are not more than two stops under or three stops over the optimum, then I shall probably be able to produce satisfactory prints. But when I use transparency films I must try to get within half a stop either side of the optimum exposure if I am to have transparencies from which I can make good colour prints. However, this is a purely personal feeling and I know that if I used an exposure meter regularly, or a camera with built-in exposure control, then I should get a much higher proportion of successful transparencies.

History of colour negative film

Historically, colour negative materials took a good deal longer to achieve general acceptance than did colour transparency films such as Kodachrome. There were a number of reasons for this – not least of which was that the early 35 mm transparency materials were a spin-off from the 16 mm amateur movie systems of the late 1930's. The first colour negative film to be sold to amateurs was launched in 1942 in the U.S. by Eastman Kodak who called it Kodacolor and made it available only in roll film sizes. There followed a period when all the processing and printing of Kodak films was done exclusively in Kodak laboratories; but following an anti-trust suit, Kodacolor and Kodachrome processing information was released to independent photofinishers in the U.S. and later throughout the world. This extension of processing facilities together with the introduction of 126 Instamatic cartridge loading cameras in 1962 resulted in a tremendous increase in the use of colour negative films by amateurs. It was not long before the volume of colour negative exposures greatly exceeded that of colour transparencies. Professional photographers also favour colour negative films if they are to produce colour prints. Professional laboratories will produce superb hand-made prints at a price: and can also make colour transparencies or black-and-white prints from colour negatives when required. Nevertheless, with the continued improvement in the quality of reversal films, it is generally agreed that for sheer excellence of quality and brilliance of reproduction no other form of colour photography surpasses the colour slide.

Masked negatives

But there are ways in which the colour negative offers advantages over the colour transparency when colour prints are the main objective. Greater exposure latitude has already been mentioned but there is another important advantage. None of the dyes used to form colour photographic images is quite as perfect as theoretical requirements demand. In other words a magenta dye should transmit all blue and red light and completely absorb any green light, but in fact there are no magenta dyes that behave so perfectly. Because of such limitations the accuracy of reproduction in colour transparencies suffers to some slight extent as a result. But there are ways of compensating or counteracting this type of deficiency. The solution depends upon the fact that only the printing characteristics matter with a negative, its visual appearance is immaterial. When you saw a processed colour negative for the first time, you almost certainly wondered for a moment why it had an overall orange appearance. It is because yellow and red masking dyes are incorporated in the layers in the form of coloured couplers in order to improve the accuracy of colour reproduction in the finished print. Coloured couplers of this kind cannot be used in transparency films because the image obtained from the camera exposure must look correct when viewed directly or by projection.

On the other hand, just to redress the balance once more, it must be recognised that over the years colour transparency films have been getting more and more accurate in their colour reproduction because of steady improvements in dyes. So now that printing materials have also improved and processing times are reduced, it may yet prove easier for the inexperienced amateur to obtain satisfactory prints directly from transparencies than to make them from colour negatives.

Since this book is concerned with colour printing it will be assumed from now on that you have either colour negatives or colour transparencies already available. Many transparency materials are processed by the film manufacturer anyhow, so their processing poses no problem. Similarly it is not really necessary for an amateur to process his colour negative films simply because he wants to make his own colour prints. In fact there is much to be said for having your negatives processed by a good photofinisher and perhaps having a set of small prints made at the same time. If you do this, it will make it much easier to decide which negatives are worth printing and how they might be cropped for the best composition.

Developing colour negatives

If you do feel that you would sometimes like to be able to develop your own negatives – in cases of urgency for example – then you will be interested in the possibility of using a chemical kit such as Photocolor II, a two solution chemistry that can be used either for developing films or papers.

Photocolor II

Photocolor II is sold as a two solution chemistry, but strictly speaking there are three solutions involved – a colour developer, a bleach-fix and a developer accelerator to be used when developing prints.

The Photocolor outfit will process Kodacolor II, Vericolor II, Fujicolor II and Sakuracolor II films – all of which are designed to suit Kodak's C41 process. As time goes on, other manufacturers may decide to produce films that are compatible with the C41 process in which case it will be possible to process them in Photocolor solutions.

Processing times with Photocolor are quite short – development only requiring 3 minutes at 36°C (97°F) and the whole processing cycle taking about 7 minutes.

Negative and transparency sizes

Some thought should be given to the size of the negatives or slides you will be using as originals from which to make your colour prints. If you have only one camera – and do not intend to buy another – then the matter has been decided, but if you do have a choice you should consider the following points.

To obtain a 10 in print from a $2\frac{1}{4}$ in (6 cm × 6 cm) square roll film negative you must make a four times linear enlargement; from a 126 or 135 negative you will need to enlarge about 8 times, but if you use a 110 size camera, your original negatives or slides will have to be enlarged some 15 times to give you an 8 in × 10 in print. Such prints from 110 size originals are likely to need a good deal of spotting because of the blemishes that will result from any dirt or marks on the negative or transparency.

Statistically, there is a very good chance that if you are a keen amateur photographer you will already be using a 35 mm camera, in which case you will have chosen a good compromise between a reasonably sized format and a handy camera.

Differences between black and white
and colour printing

It is often said that making colour prints is just as easy as making prints in black and white. This simply is not true. What is true, now that methods have been simplified and materials improved, is that the basic sequence of steps involved in exposing and developing a colour print is very much the same as is used in black and white printing and processing; with one big difference – *filtration of the printing light.*

Many beginners feel that once a correct exposing combination has been found, then provided processing remains constant, they should be able to continue making prints from any subsequent negatives or transparencies merely by changing the duration of the exposure to suit the density of each original. Unfortunately, things are not quite as simple as that.

When a black and white image is printed onto a sheet of bromide paper it is not at all important what kind of printing light is used – provided that the printing paper is sensitive to at least part of it.

Correct exposure will be made by judgment and the whole operation is uncomplicated. But a colour negative is a combination of three different images — one of them formed of yellow dye, another of magenta dye, and the third of cyan dye. (Magenta is a bluish-red colour dye discovered in 1859 and called after the battle of that name fought during that year in Northern Italy; and cyan is bluish-green in colour and is so named because of its similarity to the colour of cyanide.) These coloured negative images are each required to modulate a corresponding emulsion layer in the three-layer colour paper on which the final image will be formed. All colour papers carry three superimposed, differently sensitised emulsion layers — one is sensitive to blue light, one to green and the third to red. The yellow image in the colour negative — or the transparency as the case may be — has to modulate or regulate the amount of blue printing light that reaches every part of the picture area of the printing paper. Similarly, the magenta and cyan images in the negative or transparency regulate the green sensitive and red sensitive layers of the paper. Now this all has to be very delicately balanced if the result is not to come out too blue or too yellow, or wrong in some other way.

Variables affecting colour balance

There are a great many variables that must be countered when determining the precise colour of exposing light that is required to yield a correctly balanced colour print. Some of the more obvious factors that can cause changes, are the colour of the light when the photograph was taken, the type of enlarging light, and above all, the characteristics of the particular type of colour paper that is being used. Any of these can easily cause a significant difference in the colour balance of the final print if their influence is not compensated by suitable modification of the colour of the print exposing light.

It may be a little difficult to realise that two enlargers of apparently similar construction can be using different lamps running at different voltages so that prints made on them using the same filtration might look significantly different when processed. Even a 10 volt change in the power supply to the enlarger can result in a noticeably different print when everything else is equal.

Two ways of colour printing

Compensation for the variables already mentioned and any others can either be made by changing the relative times of three separate red, green and blue light exposures or by modulating the colour of the printing light by means of one or more filters that we call a pack.

The pros and cons of these two methods of printing are dealt with in some detail in Chapter 3, but there are several good reasons why most colour prints are now being made by a single exposure rather than by three successive exposures. The amateur who is just beginning does not want to spend too much on specialised equipment until he has more experience. So he uses a set of colour filters that can be put together to form packs in an almost unlimited range of values so that the requirements of virtually any negative/paper combination can be satisfied. Professional printers and the more advanced amateur hobbyists will invest in an enlarger with a colour head. This incorporates the means of changing the colour of the printing light through a wide range of values without the need to handle any filters at all.

Simplified processing

More than anything else, simplification of processing has encouraged the amateur to take up colour printing. Print processing times are now often less than 10 minutes with only two or three solutions involved. For example, with a three solution chemistry such as Kodak's Ektaprint 3, the time required for the wet stages of processing a print from a colour negative will be around 8 minutes, while the Cibachrome P-12 process for making prints from transparencies will take you about 12 minutes.

Processing drums

It has already been explained that all colour print materials have to be sensitive to red, green and blue light. For this reason it is impossible to carry out the early stages of print processing by inspection – another way in which making a colour print is different from making one in black and white.

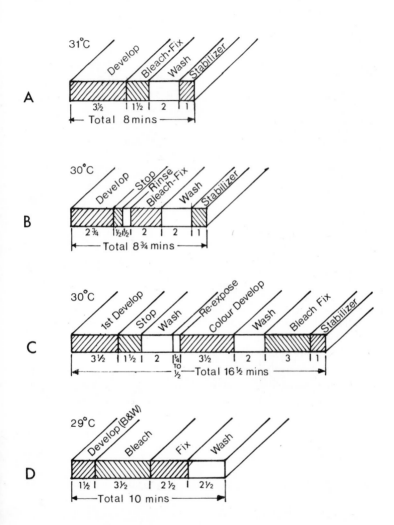

Schematic representations of steps required and total times involved for colour print processes A, Ektaprint 3. B, Agfacolor Process 85. C, Ektaprint R14. D, Cibachrome P-12.

A very low level of carefully chosen safe-lighting can be used with most colour papers, but the kind of light permitted is too little to be of much use.

One can therefore think of developing a colour print in much the same way as developing a panchromatic film. Films are usually developed in a so-called daylight tank after having been loaded into the tank in darkness. This logical idea eventually spread to colour print processing – initially with the Simmard drum – and the technique has grown so rapidly as to have transformed amateur printing. It is only fair to mention the Goodman daylight developing dish or tank which has been available for several years, but it does require rather more solution than the newer cylindrical tanks, and agitation is not so easy.

One-shot chemistry

Because very little solution is necessary when developing the print in a processing drum, it is not too expensive to use each of the processing solutions once only, pouring them away immediately after use. This form of processing, called one-shot or total loss, has the advantage of not involving any kind of replenishment or regeneration. A fresh quantity of each solution is used for every print, thereby ensuring reproducibility of processing conditions.

Of course, just as if you were developing a film in a daylight tank, the time of treatment, the temperature of the developer and the agitation must all be kept constant if you are to achieve the results you expect.

Shortened processing times

Not so long ago, it was quite usual for a colour print to require 45 minutes of wet processing, but now it is possible to get a wet print result in 10 minutes or less. This striking reduction in processing time has contributed greatly to the popularity of colour printing, because too long a wait between exposing a print and seeing the result did become frustrating after the magic of making one's first few prints had begun to wear off.

Finding the right filtration

Estimating, calculating, or even guessing the right filtration for a colour negative undoubtedly remains the most difficult part of colour printing. Opinions are still divided as to the best approach to the problem. Some people think it better to make whatever number of preliminary test strips are necessary before the final exposure is made; and this may mean two, three or even more tests for the inexperienced amateur. Others find that at least one and sometimes two testing stages can be avoided by using some kind of calculator or estimator. One thing is certain, subjective judgment must always play a significant part in the production of any really successful colour print and this kind of judgment can only come from experience, so the more colour prints you make the fewer test strips you will find you need.

Making
a
Start

This chapter is intended for those who, having decided that they would like to try their hand at making colour prints, are impatient to know what they will need and how to get started. Perhaps this is not unlike wanting to pick out a tune on a piano without having had any music lessons. Some people have the flair and can do these things; although those who play by ear are generally willing to admit later that they wish they had been taught properly. However, for those beginners who are anxious to make a colour print as soon as possible without bothering too much about achieving perfect quality, these are the basic requirements:

Basic equipment

1 Enlarger. (One with a filter drawer.)
2 Masking frame. (Enlarging easel.)
3 Set of colour printing filters. (Size to suit enlarger.)
4 Ultra-violet absorbing and heat absorbing filters.
5 Supply of colour paper.
6 Kit of chemicals to suit paper.
7 Bottles to store solutions.
8 1 litre and 100 ml plastic measuring cylinders and at least 3 × 100 ml. beakers with 50 ml markings.
9 Print processing drum.
10 Thermometer. (Range 10–50°C.)
11 Exposure timer.
12 Notebook and soft lead pencil.

If you decide to buy one of the several colour printing kits that are available, most of these things will be included. However, do find out what is in your kit, and get the remaining items before you try to start.

The size of negative the enlarger will accept and therefore the size of filter set you will need, the size of the enlarging easel, the paper and the processing drum, must all depend on your particular choice.

Additive printing

If you are thinking that there must be ways of making colour prints that require a shorter list of things than this, you are quite correct. But

If no other space is available, it is quite possible to work successfully in the bathroom. You will need to make quite sure that all daylight can be blocked out with a really tight fitting board or blind. It will also help greatly if you make a removable bench to rest over the bath and support your enlarger as well as the few other things you must have on hand.

the alternative way is less convenient and can sometimes lead to disappointing results. To print colour paper by making three separate exposures for each print certainly does enable you to work with only three filters, but you then have to be extremely careful not to move the enlarger or the negative between the three exposures. Also, as these filters are normally held below the lens, they must be of 'optical' quality, and be kept scrupulously clean. However this alternative method is described in pp. 55–60.

Processing in a dish

You can also avoid the cost of a print processing drum by working in dishes instead, but then you need to work in the dark throughout processing and it is quite difficult to maintain the solution temperature accurately enough for reproducible results.

Darkroom space

Because the number of solutions in use in colour printing is few and processing tanks or drums can, once they have been loaded, be used in daylight, the darkroom space required is not very great and should not be too difficult to find or improvise.

You do not necessarily have to use any solutions in the darkroom so there need be no danger of accidental spilling or overflow, and if all else fails a trestle table can be set up in a bedroom and dismantled after each printing session. You should allow a little more bench space than is required for the enlarger itself; because you must have somewhere to keep your filters, exposure timer, developing tank and notebook. If any of these things are too near the edge of the bench you will surely knock them off in the dark.

While it is a little more convenient to have both dry and wet sections in the same room, when this cannot be managed there is no great hardship in taking the loaded print tank to the bathroom or kitchen in order to be near a supply of water and a drain.

Make darkroom really dark

You may not appreciate that it is very difficult to make an ordinary room thoroughly light-tight. When you first enter a room that has been blacked out it may be several minutes before you come to realise that there is sufficient light for you to begin to see your way around fairly easily. So wait for ten minutes or so for your eyes to become thoroughly dark-adapted before you decide that your new darkroom is safe for handling colour paper. Then when you are satisfied that no light is leaking into the room, there will be one other test you must make, and that is to see whether any light is leaking from the lamphouse of your enlarger during exposures. This can be checked simply by putting a cap over the lens of the enlarger while it is switched on. If light does leak from any holes or gaps in the enlarger head they must either be closed or at least shielded so that no light is reflected from the wall behind or the ceiling above, otherwise your prints might well be slightly fogged.

The effects of stray light within the darkroom become noticeable when unusually long exposures are required to make big enlargements from dense negatives, but the cause of any resulting slight veiling of print highlights may then elude you for a long time; so make sure your working conditions are really safe right from the start.

Safelight

Opinions differ on the usefulness of the very low level of safelight that can be permitted with any kind of colour paper. It is not always fully realised that the emulsion used in the three layers of a colour paper have to be extremely fast and between them sensitive to all colours. In effect therefore we are handling a high speed panchromatic material and it can be argued that it is no more sensible to expect to benefit from using a safelight with colour paper than it would be if we were developing panchromatic negative material under safelight. Nevertheless, provided you are prepared to wait long enough to become thoroughly dark-adapted, then it is possible to use enough yellowish-green light to just see your way around the work bench — and this can be helpful to those who do not like feeling for everything in complete darkness.

If you are going to use Agfacolor paper you will need a very dark amber colour screen, number 08, and for Ektacolor 37 RC paper you should use a Kodak number 13 screen. These screens should be in front of a 15 watt lamp and be placed at least 30 inches from your exposing surfaces. The set-up should then be safe for periods of up to three minutes.

It is quite possible to make prints by exposing colour paper while in contact with a colour negative, thus dispensing with the enlarger – but this way of working is becoming less and less useful as negatives become smaller. It is not much good making contact prints from 110 size negatives or transparencies. It is assumed therefore that you either have an enlarger already or will be buying one. Then what kind should you buy?

The enlarger

Nearly all enlargers are now made complete with a colour filter drawer and provided that this facility is included, the other two things that will determine your choice are the size of the negatives you expect to print and the amount of money you are prepared to spend.

For the moment it will be assumed that you are not going to invest in an enlarger with a colour head incorporating a means for continuous adjustment of the ratio of red, green and blue light emerging from the lamphouse without the need for a set of separate filters. This type of colour head will be described later in the book and its advantages will then be explained.

Whatever you do spend on an enlarger, be sure to leave enough to buy a good masking board. Although not essential, there is much to be said for getting a type of enlarging easel that allows you to make four separate exposures on a single 8 in × 10 in sheet of paper.

Colour correction filters

This chapter deals with what is known as the white light or subtractive exposure method. This simply means that you will make a single exposure for each print and that the precise colour of the exposing light will be achieved by placing one or more correction filters in the light beam *before* it reaches the negative. Never put colour printing (CP), filters beneath the lens of your enlarger if you expect to get really sharp prints.

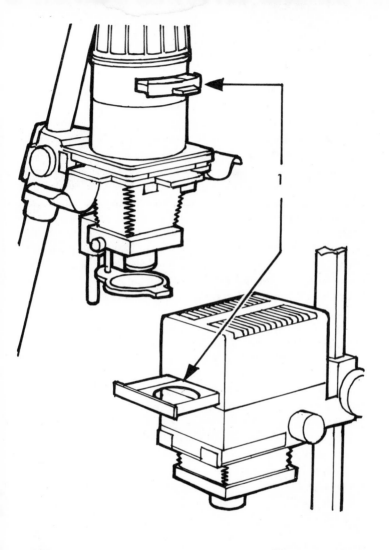

Most enlargers are now provided with a tray for holding colour correction filters. When you buy a new enlarger, check the size of the filters it takes and look to see whether it incorporates a heat absorbing glass somewhere between the lamp and the filter position.

In order to be able to assemble exactly the right combination of filters to suit any particular negative, you will find that you need quite a range in each of the three so-called subtractive primary colours, yellow, magenta and cyan.

Different manufacturers offer slightly different sets of printing filters, but typically you will get a set of twenty-one acetate or gelatin foils, seven each in yellow, magenta and cyan. Commonly the values of the seven filters range from 025 to 50 in all three colours. The meaning of the values need not concern you at the moment and until you have become acquainted with the relative effectiveness of each value of filter on the colour balance of a print, it will be enough to say that 025 is a very low density and will produce a just discernible difference in the balance of a colour print – provided nothing else changes. For beginners, the 05 filter probably represents a sufficiently sensitive adjustment while a 20 filter effects a change that is easily seen. The much denser 40 or 50 filters will not generally be required to match one negative with another of the same type, but rather to make up the basic filter pack to suit your particular enlarger and the batch of paper you happen to be using.

There are differences between the sets of filters sold by different manufacturers, but don't worry too much about this; simply choose a set and then get used to them. Never interchange filters from one manufacturer with those of another because they may well differ in colour and in density even though they are identified in the same way.

The size of the filters you buy will be governed by the filter drawer of your enlarger.

If you use 35 mm or 126 size film negatives, you may find that 3 in (7 cms) square filters will suit your enlarger, but if your negatives are larger than that you may need 5 in square filters. From this you will realise that you should not buy your filters until you are sure of your enlarger.

Heat absorbing filters

If you buy a new enlarger and it has a filter drawer, which it should have, then it is quite likely that you will find a glass heat absorbing filter already supplied in the tray. if not you will need to get a piece of heat absorbing glass cut to the right size. It can go either in the filter tray or, even better, in some permanent position just above it. Chance Bros. make heat absorbing glass called ON13, and a 2 mm thickness of the right size will serve your purpose. This glass filter is required to absorb most of the heat from the enlarger lamp that might otherwise damage your negative and your filters. A heat absorbing filter also ensures that only visible red light is recorded by the red sensitive emulsion of your colour paper. Some red sensitive emulsions can record infra-red radiation and in doing so impair the colour reproduction from your negatives or slides. If you need strong cyan filtration this usually means that you have not got a suitable heat absorbing filter in your enlarger

Ultra-violet filters

Not every paper manufacturer asks for an ultra-violet absorbing filter to be used between the light source and the negative when printing on their colour paper, but Kodak does, and since such a filter will certainly have no adverse effect on any type of paper, one should be placed in position at the outset. The recommended Kodak filter is their CP2B, and it should be permanently located in the filter drawer.

Colour papers

In this book there is no reason and no intention to recommend the use of one type of colour paper in preference to any other. All currently available papers for printing from colour negatives work in a basically similar way and have to be handled in much the same manner. One thing that can be recommended is the use of resin coated (RC) or as it is sometimes termed polyethylene (PE) coated paper. Both Kodak and Agfa, as well as other manufacturers, now supply colour paper of this type and the shortened washing and drying times that result from its use certainly make it preferable to the earlier unprotected paper base materials.

There are two principal classes of colour paper available, and in the U.S. these are grouped into Type A and Type B papers. The papers in the Type A group include Kodak Ektacolor RC 37 and some papers made by other manufacturers that are compatible with Ektaprint 3 chemistry.

The Type B papers and chemistry sold by Agfa-Gevaert are different from those of Kodak and are not therefore compatible with them.

For the moment we need not consider the points of difference between colour papers except to mention that because of the colour couplers used in their emulsion, Kodak colour papers display a milky or opalescent appearance between the wet and dry states. This characteristic difference means that a reasonably reliable judgment of colour balance can be made without waiting to dry an Agfa print or test strip, whereas it is necessary to dry Kodak colour paper before the image can be safely assessed.

Three solution processing

In recent years the principal solutions involved in colour print processing have been reduced to three:

1 Colour developer
2 Bleach-fix
3 Stabiliser

This reduction in the number of processing solutions has meant that all manufacturers of colour paper have made many alterations to their formulae and procedures during the last few years. There is no reason to suppose that further simplification will not be introduced in due course and therefore it must be realised that any specific instructions given with the paper and chemicals you use may be more recent than the processing recommendations given here, so if they differ in any way, *the information given with the materials should be used.*

Chemical mixing

For the reasons given in the preceding paragraph, whatever manufacturer's instructions are found packed with the processing chemicals you buy, they should be read carefully and strictly observed. When the complex chemical reactions involved in processing a colour print are made as simple in use as possible by formulating chemistry that involves only three working solutions, then it is sometimes necessary to ensure that a strict procedure is followed in the preparation of the working solutions.

Ektaprint 3

Chemicals for the Ektaprint 3 process are all supplied as liquid concentrates and the working solutions are therefore quite easily made up simply by dilution to larger volumes. Even so the instructions should be carefully followed.

Agfacolor 85 Kit

The one litre Agfa Process 85 kit is supplied in powder form and consists of: two packets of developer, and one packet each of stop bath, bleach-fix and final bath.
Parts A1 and A2 of the developer do not completely dissolve in the 0.8 litres of water used initially, but solution is completed when part B is added.
The final bath — a stabiliser — requires 5 ml of 30% formalin to be added before it is ready for use.

Changing papers or chemicals

Having decided on your paper you should also use the chemistry recommended for it by the manufacturer. At least to start with you do not want to find yourself wondering if some unexpected result could be due to the fact that you were using chemicals supplied by some firm other than the one that made the paper.
Although you may feel that you would like to try a variety of colour papers in due course, you are well advised to make a choice and stick to it until you have gained a good deal of experience. To change from

paper to paper while you are still learning is likely to hinder rather than help your progress.

Choosing a negative

With your solutions prepared and your equipment arranged conveniently in a well tested darkroom area, you are nearly ready to expose your first test. But before you are quite ready you must choose a colour negative to print. This choice is really very important because you expect to learn a great deal from printing this first negative, so it should represent as far as possible the kind of negatives you expect to be printing later. In other words, if you can avoid it, don't choose a negative that was made on Kodacolor X film when you will be using Kodacolor II film in future. There are differences between these two negative types that result in quite different printing filtrations.

If you can manage to do so, it will help considerably if you expose a roll of film expressly to provide a series of reference or master negatives to which you will be able to refer from time to time. By devoting a film to obtaining test negatives, you will be able to vary the exposures you give so that the negative you choose as your starting point will have been properly exposed. Furthermore, you will probably be able to see to it that there is some neutral grey in your subject area and this will help you greatly in arriving at an optimum colour print.

Colour negative processing

You need not necessarily develop your own colour negatives, because by the time a film is ready for processing the most important decisions have been taken; you have chosen your subject, decided on its composition and determined the exposure you will give. With all these variables behind you the only thing to be done to the film is to ensure that it is properly processed. While it is certainly possible for you to do this yourself there is not much fun in it and no way in which you can express any individuality, as you can when it comes to printing the negatives.

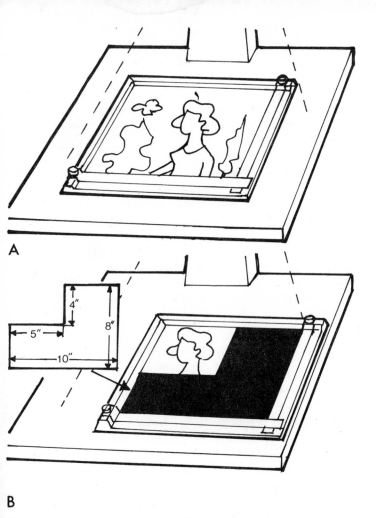

A

B

Before making a series of tests to determine either exposure time or filtration, first compose your picture in the enlarging easel, A. Then, by using a black card mask cut to the dimensions given in, B, you can turn it round and over to expose each quarter of an 8 × 10 inch sheet in turn. After each exposure, the easel must be moved so that the same area of the projected image is recorded.

41

Another factor to be considered before you embark on processing colour negatives is that the Flexicolor process (Kodacolor II) is now operated at 100°F and such a high working temperature is difficult to maintain under domestic conditions.

Therefore unless you are in a great hurry to see what you have got on the film you might just as well have it processed by a good photofinisher, who will often give a 24 hour service if you are not asking for prints. Of course you should make sure that the photofinisher you choose works to a high standard of quality and the only way to ensure this is to have him develop and print a few rolls of film before you entrust him with the shots you intend to print yourself.

If you do want to process your own films, there is available one kit of chemicals suitable both for films and papers. It is a 2-bath process called Photocolor II. It is suitable for Kodacolor II and related films and for Kodak type papers.

Even though it may take a bit longer and cost rather more, it will be as well to have prints made from your first experimental roll so that you will have some idea of the results that can be expected from the negatives.

Starting filters

Having chosen a negative to print you will need to decide on the filters you will use to start with. The starting filters recommended when using Kodacolor II negatives with a typical batch of Ektaprint 37 RC paper are 100 Y and 75 M. With a Kodacolor X negative you might start with 50 Y and 50 M.

If you are using Agfacolor CNS2 with Agfacolor MCN317 Type 4 paper, then it will be as well to start with 50 Y and 50M filters in the enlarger.

You must not assume that because these starting packs have been suggested that they will result in perfectly balanced colour prints at your first attempt. For one thing, you know nothing yet about the overall exposure you will require to obtain a print of the right density, let alone the right colour. But since you have to start somewhere these suggestions should serve your purpose.

Having placed the proposed filters into the filter drawer of your

By means of white painted light-tight hinged flaps, the Durst Comask enlarging board – A, allows four 4 × 5 inch test areas to be exposed on a sheet of 8 × 10 inch paper. Alternatively, the easel can be used to make two 5 × 8 inch prints, or one print 8 × 10 inches. The Quadrimask easel – B, serves the same purpose, but is used by changing the position of three separate 4 × 5 inch masks after each exposure.

enlarger you must now make a series of test exposures of varying duration to find out which will give you the print of the required density. These tests can be made on a single sheet of paper if it is masked successively during the series of exposures. Since it is just as easy to process a sheet of 8 in × 10 in paper as smaller sizes and since tests that are too small are apt to be misleading, you may as well make four 4 in × 5 in test exposures on the same 8 in × 10 in sheet of paper. By making four test exposures on a single sheet of 8 in × 10 in paper, you can centre the most important part of your picture area on to each quarter of the paper in turn. There are two ways of doing this, either with a specially designed masking frame such as the ones made by Durst or Quadrimask or by using an 8 in × 10 in card mask with one 4 in × 5 in corner cut out of it.

Exposure time

You can make these four tests by giving exposures of four different durations – say 5, 10, 20, and 40 seconds at the same lens aperture – say $f8$ – or you can expose each section for the same time and vary the aperture of your enlarging lens for each exposure, using for example this series of stops: $f5.6$, $f8$, $f11$ and $f16$.

Recording exposure conditions

Now is the time to establish the habit of recording on the backs of your prints and in a log book the essential details of every print you make. This practice may never make it possible for you to go back to a negative and make a first time print with exactly the same density and colour balance as you did a year ago, but by using the information in your notebook you will be able to get a good print with less testing than if you have to start from the beginning again.

It needs a very soft lead pencil to write on the back of a print and the writing should be done immediately after you take the exposed sheet from the enlarger board. If you were working from a Kodacolor II negative the kind of information you would write on the very first test would be 100 Y, 50 M, 10 secs, $f5.6$–8–11–16. Additional informa-

Date	Type of Film	Number or Description of Neg or Slide	Enlargement Ratio	Lens Aperture
4/1/75	KODACOLOR II	DUTCH BARGE – AMSTERDAM '74'	6x	f6·3
"	"	REPEAT	"	"
"	"	FINAL PRINT	"	"
	KODACOLOR X	MARY ON BEACH SC...	5x	f6·3

Filters Y – M – C	Exposure Time	Description of Result
120 – 60 – 0	6 SECS. 12 " 24 " 48 "	12 SECS CORRECT – COLOUR – MUCH TO BLUE. TRY — 12 SECS 80-50-0 60-50-0
80 – 50 – 0 60 – 50 – 0	12 SECS	80 - 50 - 0 O.K.
80 – 50 – 0	"	NOT BAD!
80 – 50 – 0	6 – 12 – 24 – 48 SECS	10 SECS ABOUT RIGHT

It is always worth while to keep a log of all the test strips and prints you produce. You will be surprised how often you find yourself uncertain of the filtration or the exposure you used for a test. Unless you record the details, preferably before each exposure, you will surely waste a lot of time and sometimes end up with puzzling results.

tion such as the paper batch number and the enlargement ratio should be included in your notebook, which may need to be ruled off across two pages to allow for all the information you need to record.

Print processing

So now you are ready to process your first sheet of colour paper. But before you can do so, you must prepare the solutions you will need in the volumes recommended for an 8 in × 10 in print in your particular drum. The temperature you will work at and the way you achieve it will again depend on the recommendations given for the drum you are using. If it is a Simmard drum you will need to know the temperature recommended by the manufacturer of the paper and the temperature in your workroom. Knowing these two things, you can use a nomograph provided by Simmard to find what temperature the pre-soak and wash water must be. If you are using a Kodak Printank with Ektaprint 3 chemistry, you will need a bowl of water at 32°C in which to float the drum throughout the development period. Other systems have their own temperature control recommendations. They all work well if followed exactly.

Loading paper into drum

Placing an exposed sheet of 8 in × 10 in paper into a drum is not very difficult to do in the dark, but it will be made that much easier to carry out if you have done it a few times previously in white-light – using a scrap piece of paper.

Processing drums vary in their design, and while some of them have removable dividers or separators, others have a perfectly smooth inner wall. Whichever type you have, make sure that the exposed sheet is inserted symmetrically, so that there is no overlap or interference with the lid when it is screwed or pressed on to the end of the tank. Most people cannot wait until the complete processing cycle is finished before removing the print to see what it is like. If you are impatient too, then the end cap can be removed from the drum after the bleach-fixing is complete and the residual bleach fix solution has been washed away.

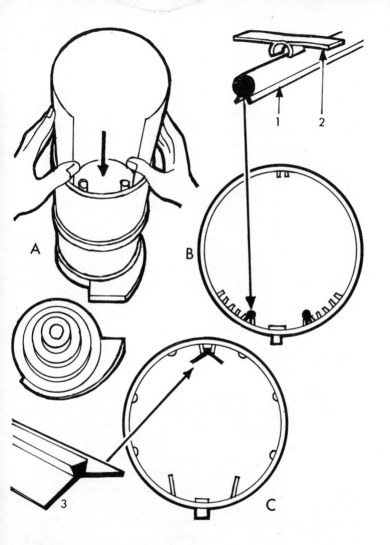

By holding an exposed sheet of paper in the way shown in A, it is easier to guide it into position in the processing drum. "Wing" – shaped print separator – C3, were used in earlier Simmard drums, but sometimes caused edge effects on processed prints. They have been superseded by round section "cling-flow" separators – B1 and 2, that do not cause uneven processing and are easier to clean.

Getting density right

When you have looked at the print you will soon be able to tell whether any one of the four images seems to be about right for density. If you are using Ektaprint RC paper the wet print will have a bluish opalescent appearance so that you cannot tell much about its colour while it is wet. Unless the negative you choose is unusually thin or dense or your enlarger has an extremely low or high light output, you should find that one of the four quarters of the test print will be about right for density even though it may be a long way off for colour. So the next test you make should be aimed at getting much nearer to correct colour balance and the four test sections can therefore be devoted to trying four different filter packs.

This procedure, whereby correct density is achieved before paying attention to colour balance is quite important. Don't try to adjust your colour and density at the same time because you will find it much easier – at least while you are learning – to deal with these variables in turn.

Getting colour right

Now you have reached the heart of this business of colour printing. You have a test print of about the right density, but the wrong colour. You know the colour is wrong, but without experience you will probably feel quite uncertain what should be done to make it right. Without describing just what happens in the three layers of a colour paper when it is exposed to an image of a colour negative – something we will leave to a later chapter – you need to know and remember that with the negative/positive process any excess of one colour is reduced by the addition of correction filters of that same colour. In other words, if your print is obviously too yellow then you will make the next print after adding more yellow to the filter pack. Yes, you will be thinking, but how much extra yellow. And here is the rub. The more experienced you become the more sure you will be, after looking at a test, just what changes in filtration will be necessary to bring the print on balance. But while you are learning, the best way to work, is to compare your test print with the 'ring around' pictures on p. 102.

As a rough guide a just noticeable colour bias requires a 10 filter or pair of 10 filters of the appropriate colours; a more obvious shift may be compensated by denser filters valued 20 or 30, while a very large correction may require 40, 50 or more.

Adjusting exposure

One more point. When you have decided on the modification you will make to the filter pack before exposing the next test, remember that increasing the density of the pack will necessitate some increase in overall exposure. Conversely, if you reduce its density, then the next exposure should be less. As a rough guide, the addition of each additional filter (of whatever density) requires an increase in exposure of about 10%. In the same way, if the number of filters remains the same but the density of any of them is increased, then this alteration also calls for an increase in exposure. The necessary increase varies according to the colour and density of the additional filtration. It can be as much as 60% for an extra 50 C, and you may even have to double the previous exposure if you add 50 M.

So how do you calculate the new exposure? Use the information supplied by the filter manufacturer. This may be tables of exposure factors, or a simile rotary or sliding calculator.

By now you will be wondering whether there are some short cuts in colour printing. There are a few, which will be discussed later, but the fact remains that a skilled colour printer is one who has made a lot of prints and a great many more test strips. So give yourself time to decide as carefully as you can what changes to make in filtration and then, after recording that in your log book make another test print, process it *exactly* as before and see how much nearer you get this time.

You can take some comfort from the fact that beginners are usually much more tolerant of the quality of their first few prints than they ever are when they become more experienced, and you will probably be delighted with your first results.

Printing from transparencies

The whole of this chapter has been written on the assumption that you want to make colour prints from colour negatives. If instead you really want prints from your colour slides then you need to use a colour paper intended for reversal processing and then your colour correction will be done by using filters complimentary to any excess colour in the print, while you would make a print lighter by giving it more exposure. All of these differences are explained on pp. 149–172.

Methods
of
Exposure

If, after reading the previous two chapters, you have decided to make yourself a colour print even though you were given limited information and guidance, you will quickly come to realise that the hardest part of colour printing lies in determining the exposure time and colour corrections required for each new negative. So we should now spend rather more time looking at some of the factors that have a bearing on this central problem.

Already you are probably wondering why it is that you cannot expose all your colour negatives with the same filter pack provided you use the same batch of colour paper.

Reasons for differences

In practice, there are several variables that can cause sufficient differences between negatives to necessitate the use of different filtration when they are printed — even though they may look the same.

First of all, no manufacturer can make colour negative material without some batch to batch variations. Although such variations cannot usually be detected by looking at negatives, they can be sufficient to cause differences between prints. The first maxim therefore is to buy as many films as you can manage at one time, and to ensure that they all have the same batch number.

The conditions under which you store your films, either before or after exposure, can also result in changes in performance at the printing stage. So keep your film in a refrigerator and keep your camera away from very hot or humid places. Unexposed film is sensitive enough to adverse conditions; but exposed unprocessed (latent) images deteriorate even faster.

Processing variations

Even more significant are the variations in processing that result when films are developed at different times and by different people. It is therefore essential to ensure that your negatives are processed correctly. Really keen amateurs who have time may take the view that the safest way is to develop their own negatives; but not only is this a somewhat expensive solution to the problem, it is becoming increasingly difficult for the amateur to manage it since processing temperatures for films such as Kodacolor II have been set as high as 100°F and this can easily lead to variable quality.

A good photofinisher has the means and the staff at his disposal to make a sound job of processing colour negative films and provided you regularly check on the quality of the prints he produces, you should feel quite happy to entrust your negatives to a local laboratory. There are many small laboratories catering mainly for professionals. Some of these take single films or small batches from amateurs directly. Alternatively, you may find a local wedding and portrait photographer willing to include your films with his laboratory order, or a photographic dealer who has a regular service from a 'professional' laboratory. These laboratories usually process to a high standard, are often quicker than normal photofinishers, and they process films without expecting to make prints. Their 'process only' charges are usually quite reasonable, but their (normally extremely good) colour printing costs may be staggeringly high.

The third major variable is up to you. Like any other film, colour negative materials yield best results when they are consistently exposed. Extreme differences in exposure can produce colour balance changes as well as density variations.

What happens

To better understand how any of these variations can affect the printing characteristics of a colour negative we should consider what happens when the image of a colour negative is projected onto a sheet of colour paper.

Any colour negative film consists of three superimposed emulsion layers, each made sensitive to only one of the three primary colours — blue, green and red. Upon exposure to a scene, all the red light reflected from the subject is recorded by the bottom layer of the film, all the green light from the subject is caught by the middle (green sensitive) layer, while the blue content of the scene is recorded by the blue sensitive emulsion on the top.

During processing these three different records of the same subject are treated in a developer that not only forms silver images but also forms a corresponding yellow dye image in the top layer, a magenta image in the middle and a cyan (bluish-green) image in the bottom layer. After all the silver has been bleached out of the three emulsion layers, the subtractive or 'minus' colour images remain. They serve just as well as silver images to control the passage of blue, green or red light and therefore represent – in negative values – the blue, green and red contents of the original scene.

This colour negative can now be used to project suitably modulated blue, green and red light to form an image on a sheet of colour paper. This paper also carries three superimposed blue, green and red sensitive emulsion layers.

To complete the sequence, the latent images formed in the three layers of the colour paper are developed in much the same way as the negative was developed. Silver images are formed together with yellow, magenta and cyan images representing blue, green and red records of the original subject. This time the images are positive in value and after all the unwanted silver has been removed the composite colour picture is complete.

Imagine a perfectly neutral object, such as a white painted pyramid or cylinder placed against a background of white paper. It is seen as a variety of neutral greys, varying in density according to the direction of light. Suppose we take a picture of this set-up on a colour negative film and print it onto colour paper. The three images formed in the negative and the three subsequently formed in the print should all be equal in their ability to modulate or absorb the blue, green and red rays contained firstly in the printing light and then in the reflected light by which we view the print.

Such perfect control of photographic manufacture and processing is beyond everyday achievement because small divergencies inevitably creep in at one point or another and some colour adjustment usually becomes necessary when the print is made. This is why there is always so much talk of colour correction, filter packs and colour mixing heads when you make colour prints.

Colour correction masking dyes

Having explained all this, you will probably be wondering why it is that all the colour negatives you have seen have looked far from neutral grey and instead have an overall orange/red appearance. Don't let this confuse you. The orange appearance is to do with colour correction or masking dyes that serve to improve the hue of the magenta and cyan images and have nothing to do with the balance of the three component images of the negative.

Reference or standard negatives

Early on in your attempts to improve the quality of your colour prints you should take the trouble to expose a roll of colour negative film with the express purpose of making some standard or reference negatives. To have one or two negatives that you know can produce really high quality prints is tremendously important, because whenever you are wondering why you are finding it difficult to obtain a good result from a particular negative, a print made from one of your reference negatives will quickly tell you whether your paper and your paper processing are in order and if so, that there is something amiss with your troublesome negative.

If you decide to have your reference negatives processed by a photofinisher, then get him to make a few prints at the same time. These prints will give you a pretty good idea of the kind of results you can expect to get when you come to print the negatives yourself. Of course you may be able to do better than the photofinisher, but his prints will generally serve as a useful guide.

The type of subject you choose to photograph for your standard negatives must depend on the kind of photography you expect to do. It is always useful to include some neutral greys as well as a range of bright colours. If you expect to print a lot of portrait or wedding pictures, then you should use one of these subjects for your reference negative.

Tricolor additive exposures

A simple way of adjusting the relative densities formed in the blue, green and red sensitive layers of a sheet of colour paper is to give the three layers separate exposures through blue, green and red filters. You adjust the times of the three exposures to achieve a balanced colour image. However, if you work this way you have to be careful to avoid the slightest movement of either the enlarger or the printing paper between exposures. Furthermore, dodging or burning in local areas of the image while exposure proceeds is extremely difficult. This facility, which makes black and white printing so interesting, is much simpler and can be more subtle if a single subtractive exposure is made onto the colour paper.

Despite the disadvantages, you may want to start colour printing this way because you don't need a new enlarger, and you only have to buy the filters.

Tricolor filters

You need primary red, blue and green filters. These are often sold as sets for colour printing. The exact colours are not critical, but you must always use the same make if you want repeatable results. Quite small (50 × 50 mm) gelatin filters are suitable, but they must be of good optical quality like those used on camera lenses.

For each of the three exposures you hold one of the filters below the lens. To make things easier, you can construct a simple card mount to fit your enlarger. Because the image is formed through them, it is vitally important that the filters never get scratched or dirty. When you first buy your set of filters, put a strip of adhesive tape along one edge of each. Always hold the filters by this strip *alone*. Cut identification notches in the strip, so that you can tell the colours in the dark.

Test prints

Just as with subtractive printing, you can make four tests on a sheet of 8 in × 10 in paper. Take special care to record everything you do, so that you can see immediately the exposures needed to give you the print you want. Make quite sure that you measure times exactly, otherwise you can't work out reliable exposures.

Set up your enlarger for the picture size you want, and focus a suitable part of the negative on one quarter of the frame. Turn out the lights, and expose the first corner of your test sheet.

Set your enlarger lens to about f5.6. First give an overall exposure of 5 seconds through the *blue* filter. Then make three stepped exposures

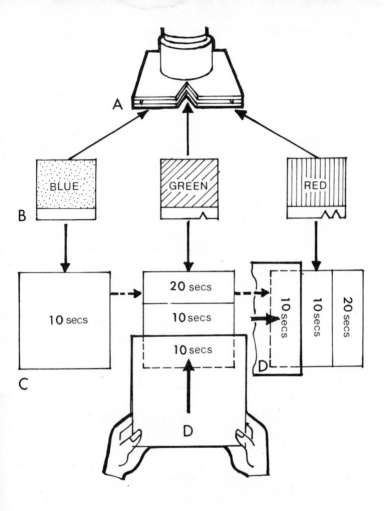

Here is a way of making preliminary test exposures by the additive printing method. With a filter holder or slide attached to the enlarger lens – A, first use the blue filter – B, to expose the whole of the test strip – C, for 10 seconds. Then, having changed to the green filter, use an opaque mask – D, to give sections of the paper different exposures as shown, this gives 10, 20, and 40 seconds. Turn the mask through 90° change to the red filter, and make a further set of exposures. Repeat the green and red series on the new test prints with 20 and 40 second blue exposure overall.

from top to bottom through the *green* filter. Use a piece of card to cover first one third, then two thirds of the paper to give exposures of 10, 20 and 40 seconds.

Repeat this procedure through the *red* filter, this time making the exposures progressively from side to side of the test area. You now have nine different red/green exposure combinations with a 5 second blue exposure.

Turn round the frame, and change your masking so that you can expose the next quarter of the paper. Give a 10 second exposure through the blue filter, and make a red and green exposure grid just as before. Repeat the process for 20 second and 40 second blue exposures for the other two test prints.

Process the whole sheet carefully, and when it is dry, you can find out the exposures you need to make a final print.

Choosing the colour

At least one of your four grids should have one section with more or less the correct colour balance. This gives you the times you need for a print. If your record system is awry, you can work out what the exposures were by looking at the prints. Progressively longer exposures make the prints denser. Longer *blue* exposures make them more yellow; longer *green* exposures more magenta; and longer *red* ones more cyan.

If you think that two of your segments 'straddle' the best colour and density, the optimum exposure falls between the two. For example, if the best *colour* is on the 20 second blue square halfway between the 10 seconds red/10 seconds green, and the 20 seconds green segments, make your print with 10 seconds blue, 15 seconds red and 20 seconds green.

Density

The segment (or pair of segments) giving the colour you want may not be the right density. To change the density, you must change all three exposures by the same proportion. Increase exposure time to make a denser print, decrease it to make a paler one.

For example, suppose 20 seconds blue, 10 seconds green and 15 seconds red appears to give the correct colour, but do not produce a dark enough print. To increase the density give (say) 30 seconds blue, 15 seconds green and 22½ seconds red.

Comparing your four tests should show you by how much you need to alter the exposure. In fact, each one should have one segment more or less the right colour, increasing in density as the exposures were increased.

Alternatively, you may find it simpler to alter the density by changing your lens aperture, so that you can use the exposure times you calculated to give the optimum colour balance. Never alter the aperture during the series of exposures. Not only will this make calculation extremely difficult, you may alter the focus or move the image slightly.

Making a print

Once you have worked out the three exposures, you are ready to make your print. Check your enlarger is still focused, make your three exposures and process the print.

It should come out just as you want it. However, when you see the whole print (perhaps mounted or in different lighting) you may still not be satisfied.

Fine adjustments

In another print, you can alter the colour and density exactly as you wish, just by changing the exposure times through the filters. Increasing the relative exposure time decreases the colour in the print, and vice versa. Thus, giving more exposure through the red filter makes the print more cyan (less red), and decreasing it makes it more red; and so on.

Naturally, altering the exposure through any filter alters the overall density, you must alter the exposure through all three filters. However, for slight alterations, you can change the exposure through one filter by up to about 20 per cent without noticeably affecting the density.

COLOUR CORRECTIONS WITH TRICOLOR PRINTING

Print colour	Cause	Changes needed
Too Cyan	Red exposure too long	Reduce red exposure
Too Magenta	Green exposure too long	Reduce green exposure
Too Yellow	Blue exposure too long	Reduce blue exposure
Too Red	Red exposure too short	Increase red exposure
Too Green	Green exposure too short	Increase green exposure
Too blue	Blue exposure too short	Increase blue exposure

Further prints

Once you have made prints from a few negatives, you will know more or less what exposures you need. You can then reduce the spread of your tests. For example your blue exposure is always between about 18 and 23 seconds, you can make your four tests at 15, 18, 22 and 25 seconds – with a suitably short series of green and red exposure times. Or perhaps you can get close enough to make just two test grids – so testing two negatives on each piece of 8 in × 10 in paper.

Naturally, if you need especially long or especially short exposures, you can alter your lens aperture to suit. However, once you have chosen an aperture, always use that aperture for your test grids. Otherwise you may get confused.

Changing to subtractive printing

Additive colour printing is rather fiddly, and creative effects are limited. However, it does let you make top quality prints with little equipment; and, perhaps more important, it lets you try out the processing techniques.

Once you have mastered the processing, you can always change to subtractive printing when you find the additive method cramps your style. You will have the processing equipment, and so have spread your outlay.

Subtractive colour correction

Suppose a print of a neutral subject turns out to be too yellow. Then for some reason or other a disproportionally large amount of yellow dye has been formed in the blue-sensitive layer of the paper. In other words, this layer received too much exposure when the print was made.

So how shall we change this when we make the next print? We know that we must reduce the exposure of the yellow image layer and since this emulsion is sensitive only to blue light we can easily do this if we subtract, or absorb, some blue from the printing light. The easiest way of doing this is to insert a suitable yellow filter into the printing beam.

The example of a print that is too yellow is a simple one, and obviously a colour print can have a colour cast or bias in any one of six different directions according to whether there is an excess of only one of the subtractive colours – yellow, magenta or cyan – or too much of any combination of any two of these three dyes. For instance, the print may be too red, in which case it has too much yellow and too much magenta dye, so besides the yellow filter necessary to reduce the exposure of the blue sensitive layer we shall also need a magenta filter to absorb some green light and thereby reduce the exposure and consequent density of the green sensitive, magenta forming, layer of the paper.

Of course there can be times when a print displays an excess of all three subtractive colours, but this is simply another way of saying that the print is too dark, a condition that can easily be corrected by reducing the printing exposure. There is hardly ever any need to use filters of all three subtractive colours at the same time, since if you do, you are certainly adding some grey density and therefore prolonging exposure unnecessarily.

It is very easy to describe colour correction filters in terms such as pale yellow or low density magenta, but finding just the right combination of filter colours and densities to suit a particular negative is the trickiest part of colour printing. While experience is really the only answer to this problem there are ways in which print exposures can be estimated with some degree of accuracy and some of these procedures will be described later.

Enlargers for colour printing

The essential requirements for an enlarger that will be used to expose colour paper by the subtractive method are that the lamphouse is perfectly light tight and that it should have either a filter drawer or a colour mixing head. A filter tray is provided with most enlargers these days and it should be located between the lamp and the negative.

Theoretically it makes no difference where the filters are located — they could be between the lamp and the negative, between the negative and the lens or between the lens and the printing paper — but in practice the best place is in the lamphouse between the lamp and the negative because here the physical condition of the filters is not very important. If there are scratches or fingerprints on them neither of these blemishes will affect the quality of the resulting print. Any filters that are used between the negative and the lens or between the lens and the paper must be optically perfect if they are not to impair the quality of the projected image. Not only must they be free from scratches and fingermarks, but they must also be of specially made 'optical' quality and are known as colour correction or CC filters.

Condenser or Diffuser?

Apart from deciding on the range of negative sizes you want to print, a choice will also have to be made between those enlargers with a condenser in the optical system and those which use diffused light to illuminate the negative or transparency. Either of these types of enlarger provide enough light to print modern colour papers at conveniently short times of exposure. So there is no need to use a condenser system just because of its greater light efficiency. The principal disadvantage of using specular illumination (such as that from condensers) is that all negative defects are imaged clearly on the print. So spotting and retouching are almost a necessity. With diffused light most scratches and dust specks will escape being printed. For this reason, therefore, it is better to choose an enlarger with diffuse illumination. Whatever type of enlarger is used it should include a heat absorbing glass to protect the filters you will be using to correct colour balance.

Kodak filters

Kodak distinguish between colour printing (CP) filters made from acetate sheet and their high quality gelatine colour compensating (CC) filters, which can if necessary be used beneath the lens of an enlarger. The printing filters are made in yellow, magenta and cyan as well as red. The red filters can take the place of equivalent values of yellow and magenta, thereby replacing two filters by one to simplify the filter pack.

The values of the CP colour range are: 05, 10, 20, 40, in cyan, magenta, yellow and red plus an 025 cyan and an 80 yellow and red.

The smallest size is 7 × 7 cm square and this will be large enough for most amateur requirements.

Colour compensating filters are sold in 05, 10, 20, 30, 40 and 50 in each of cyan, magenta, yellow, red, green and blue.

Agfa filters

The colour printing filters supplied by Agfa come either as plain gelatine foils or bound between glass. In either form they are made in two sizes – 7 cm square or 12 cm square, the former intended for 6 × 6 enlargers and the other for 6 × 9 enlargers.

All the Agfa filter sets comprise yellow, magenta and cyan filters in these density values: 05, 10, 20, 30, 40, 50 and two valued at 99 or a nominal 100.

The glass bound sets of filters are exactly the same in value but in use, these filters, because of the four additional glass/air surfaces, require slightly higher exposure factors than the plain gelatine set.

Other filter sets

Besides those made by Kodak and Agfa, sets of colour printing filters are supplied by manufacturers such as Beseler, Ciba-Geigy, GAF, Unicolor and others. If you decide to use one of these sets, do not suppose that they are interchangeable with other manufacturers' filters any more than Kodak and Agfa filters are directly interchangeable. In other words, stick to the filters you originally chose, or change the complete set. By way of an example of the differences that may be involved, you can take it that Kodak filters are denser than Agfa filters of the same nominal values. The ratio is approximately 1 : 1.35, in other words, a Kodak CP30 is the equivalent of an Agfa 40.

Care and identification of filters

Even though small superficial defects on colour printing filters will not be imaged on a print if the filter is located between the lamp and the negative, this is no reason for being careless with your filters. For one thing, they are quite expensive and therefore should be handled and stored carefully. A box with sections or divisions for your yellow, magenta, cyan and possibly red filters will allow you easily to locate the ones you want.

Some suppliers sell their filters in quite convenient folders or swatches, but however you keep them, you should religiously replace each filter in its correct place as soon as you have finished with it. This way you are much less likely to make mistakes and your filters will certainly last longer.

To identify each filter, if the manufacturer has not already done so, you can either mark its value along one edge in india ink, or even better, prepare self-adhesive embossed plastic (Dymo) labels for each value and colour and place a label along the edge of each filter. This method of identification has the advantage that the label stiffens the edge of the filter and makes it easier to handle.

Filter fading

Because they are located so near to the lamp the filters you use most frequently may fade in due course. If any such change were to go unnoticed, you would eventually find yourself confused because of the anomalous results you would be getting – particularly if you tried to relate current filtration with some of your earlier printing records.

So keep a good look out for any signs that fading has started. It is quite easy to detect if you regularly lay out your filters – particularly

N 05 CYAN

Colour correction filters are quite expensive and they can easily become scratched and dirty if they are not stored carefully. One way of making filters easy to identify and easier to handle is to attach an appropriately stamped strip of embossed lettering along one edge of each foil, as shown in A. B, C, and D are suggested ways of storing your filters so they will be easily accessible.

the low density values – on a clean sheet of white paper. If there is any fading you are likely to see a central patch that is ever so slightly lighter than the corners of the filter.

Colour mixing heads

Colour printing by the subtractive method has increased in popularity and more and more professional and commercial photography involves the production of colour prints. So alternatives have been developed to the rather inconvenient method of adjusting colour balance by adding or subtracting separate filters to a filter pack housed in a drawer in the enlarger head.

Agfa colour head

Agfa was quick to perceive the problem and they produced a special lamphouse that afforded continuous alteration of filtration by adjustment of three rotary knobs and dials. The Agfa colour head was and is made primarily to fit the Agfa Varioscop enlarger, but thousands of these lamphouses are used on many other kinds of enlarger.

The Agfa colour head has an illumination system which focuses the light from a projector lamp into a small concentrated beam, at which position three annular filters are located. The filters, which are in glass are of course yellow, magenta and cyan and their densities vary from 0–100. The desired value of any of these filters can be introduced into the light beam simply by adjusting the appropriate knob and observing the corresponding scale on the front of the colour head. Additional filters have fixed values of 100 and can be added to the system so that the total available density range is 200 for each subtractive colour.

Other colour heads

Many other kinds of colour mixing heads have been designed by such manufacturers as Simmons, Durst, Beseler and others, but a new

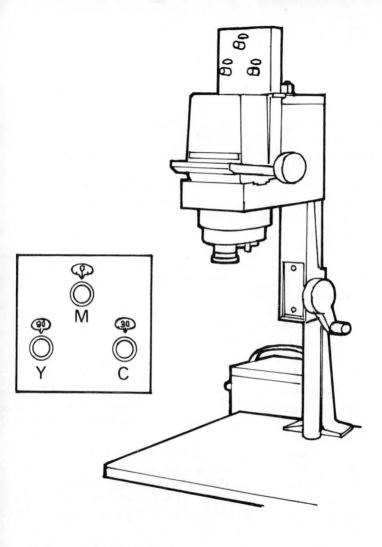

There are several different Durst enlargers available with dichroic colour heads. The one illustrated, is the M301, designed for printing 35 mm, 126 and 110 size negatives. Filtration is adjusted by means of the CLS 35 colour head with a filter range of 0 to 100 for each of the three colours.

principle was adopted when Pavelle — now Durst — first introduced their model 400 enlarger and colour head in 1962. This Pavelle head, and the many others that have followed with similar designs, is simplicity itself.

Light from a tungsten halogen lamp with an integral reflector is focused onto a small area, at which point three interference or dichroic filters can be moved into the beam. The extent to which each of the filters does in fact interrupt the beam determines the effective filter density for that position. For example, if the density of the cyan filter is 100 C and if it is placed half way into the light beam, then the colour is changed to the extent it would be by a 50 C filter.

The filtered and unfiltered components of the light beam are thoroughly scrambled in a white sided mixing box so that the negative is illuminated uniformly.

Interference or dichroic filters

Dichroic filters are glass filters on which a sequence of extremely thin and specially chosen reflective layers have been deposited in such a way as to reflect certain parts of the spectrum of light while transmitting the remainder. These interference filters can be made more efficient than dyed filters because they have no unwanted absorptions. As the deposited reflective layers are usually metals, they do not fade, and quite small areas can be safely introduced into concentrated beams of light.

A lamphouse containing the optical and mechanical requirements for a continuously variable filter adjustment costs a good deal more than one which simply incorporates a filter drawer. Nevertheless, among other manufacturers. Durst now offer a range of colour heads that are intended for use by the keen amateur or hobbyist. The smallest of these, the M301 with the CLS 35 colour mixing head, is for making colour prints from 35 mm or 126 negatives and with an additional negative holder can be used for the 110 format. As with the earlier Pavelle models, each of the three adjustment knobs on the Durst colour mixing head moves a yellow, magenta or cyan filter into the light path to produce any combination of filter densities between

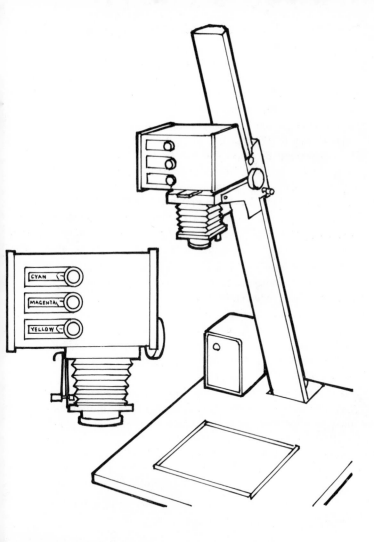

The labels on the filter head read:

CYAN

MAGENTA

YELLOW

The Chromega B enlarger will accept all negative sizes up to 6 cm. square and is equipped with a dichroic filter head. The colour of the light reaching the negative is simply and reproducibly adjusted by means of the controls on the front of the lamphouse. A range of 0–170 is available for all three colours. Unfiltered light for composing and focusing can be obtained without disturbing previous filter settings.

0–100. The chosen settings are read from three scales on the front face of the enlarger.

Usually, spring loaded or weighted cams are used in the adjustment of filters in a colour head because it is important that there should be no slackness or backlash in the mechanism used to set the filters.

Another colour head that will not be beyond the reach of some amateurs is the Simmons Chromega B, designed to handle negatives from 110 up to 2¼ in × 2¼ in.

The Chromega B lamphouse can be fitted to the Simmon B-22 enlarger and no doubt, with suitable adaptation, to a number of other types of enlarger. This lamphouse uses dichroics and has a wide range of filtration — from 0 to 170 in each of the subtractive primary colours. A 27 volt, 75 watt quartz halogen lamp provides the source of light and its output is extremely uniform throughout an estimated life of 50 hours. Both infrared and ultraviolet absorbing filters are built into this lamphouse.

To sum up, the advantages of using a colour mixing head rather than a filter pack are firstly that an infinite number of filter combinations can be achieved and any one of them can be set in moments with a high degree of accuracy, and secondly when dichroic filters are incorporated they have no unwanted absorption and therefore do not require so much additional exposure when used in high densities. Finally, unlike dyed filters, dichroic filters never fade.

Nearly all colour mixing heads use tungsten halogen lamps which have the useful property of not changing colour or brightness when used. The light emitted by an ordinary lamp becomes gradually redder and lower in intensity as it is used. Although this change is slow, it can cause abrupt differences when the time eventually comes to replace the lamp.

Voltage control

The light from an incandescent filament lamp changes colour as the voltage supplied to it varies. As the voltage drops so the relative amounts of blue light is less and red light more, which of course has much the same effect as changing the filter pack if you are exposing a colour print.

There are two ways of dealing with this problem — one requires that you watch the supply voltage and adjust it when necessary and the other is a fit and forget solution requiring a constant voltage transformer (see p. 140).

Your first exposure

The first test you make using one of your reference negatives will necessarily be something of a gamble. Initially you need to get the density of the print reasonably correct, so the first exposures should cover a fairly wide range of times — say 5–10–15–20 seconds at f8. These four test exposures can be made by uncovering successive quarters of the sheet of paper or by using a masking frame with four hinged flaps. Don't make the mistake of trying to manage with very small pieces of paper for if you do you will often be uncertain of the corrective steps you need to make because the test does not include enough of the picture.

Starting filters

Some people claim that you will do better by starting from scratch with no filters in the enlarger. However, since you are very likely to be printing from Kodacolor II negatives, you will find that if no filtration is used your first test will be very orange indeed. As a suggestion, the starting filtration when printing a Kodacolor II onto Ektacolor 37 RC paper might be 100 Y and 75 M or if you have red filters, 75 R and 25 Y.

This large amount of yellow filtration became necessary when the orange/red masking density of the older film — Kodacolor X, was replaced with the yellower mask colour of Kodacolor II. It is generally thought that in due course Kodak will modify the relative sensitivities of the emulsion layers of their colour paper so that lower and better balanced filter values will be possible when printing from Kodacolor II negatives, but for the present we must accept the situation as it is. Kodak supply 80 R and 80 Y CP filters to ease the problem.

Typically, you may find that whenever you need to print Kodacolor X negatives a filter pack containing 50 Y and 40 M will yield a test print that is not too far out.

Record exposure details

Before processing any test print, remember to enter the exposure and filter details in a log book and to identify the individual test areas by writing the information on the back of the paper with a soft lead pencil. This has to be done in the dark but it is not too difficult and you will soon learn to manage it. At first you may tend not to take this recording business seriously, but if you don't, it will not be long before you wish you had, when you cannot remember the exposure times or filtration of some negative you need to print again.

In Europe, largely because of the influence of Agfa, the accepted way of recording the details of filtration is to state them in the sequence yellow, magenta, cyan, so that a filter pack comprising 80 Y, and 60 M would be written: 80–60–00, or even more briefly: 80 60 –. A pack composed of 20 M and 10 C would then be: – 20 10.

The Kodak companies – for reasons best known to themselves, prefer to state filtration values in the order of magenta, yellow, cyan, which can sometimes lead to mistakes if one has been using the long-established Agfa procedure. The sequence: yellow–magenta–cyan will be used throughout this book.

Compare speed of bromide paper

When your first set of exposure tests has been processed there will probably be one section that is reasonably right for density; if not and all the test areas are either too light or too dark then there will be nothing for it but to repeat the test. To get a darker print you can either lengthen the time of exposure or use a larger aperture for the enlarger lens. If the exposure time looks like being longer than 20 seconds when printing your properly exposed reference negative, then you should open up the aperture of the enlarger lens, although this should never be used fully open because then there would probably be too little depth of focus at the paper plane. To make a print lighter by reducing exposure is easy enough because there is seldom any disadvantage in reducing the aperture of the lens.

By the time you have made a second set of tests you will certainly know the exposure you need but not the colour correction.

Evaluation and correction of tests and prints

No matter whether you use a filter pack or a colour mixing head you will always have to decide whether the colour balance of any test or any print you make is satisfactory and if not what changes should be made to produce a better result.

It has already been stressed that there is really only one way to become proficient at this very important business of evaluating a test or a print and deciding what changes should be made, and that is to make lots of tests and many prints. When you first tackle the job it may seem rather like tuning a violin for the first time – you know that it is out of tune yet you cannot be certain just how much to turn the keys to get each string into tune. Later when you have had more experience the whole thing becomes much easier and you will do it with confidence.

To help you while you are quite new to the task, a wide range of tests – often called a ring-around – of the same subject has been printed on page 102, to show, as far as possible with printed reproduction, just what effect different values of filtration have on a print. In broad terms these are the rules:

1 A predominant colour cast in a print is removed by adding a filter (or filters) of that same colour to the filter pack. Or, whenever it is possible, by removing filters that are complementary to the colour cast.

2 Slight colour casts require the addition or subtraction of low density filters, while more severe casts necessitate higher density changes.

3 Overcorrection results from using filters of too high a density resulting in a colour cast complementary to the original one.

4 Every additional filter increases the exposure time and the denser

the filter the greater the increase. Conversely, removing filters from the pack will reduce the necessary exposure.

5 For equivalent values, yellow filters increase exposures least and cyan increases them most.

6 Whenever possible, examine tests and prints in daylight or under special colour matching fluorescent lights.

You may find that printing your own ring-around (from a suitable negative) gives you a more suitable standard. Also, the actual printing provides very good practice in manipulating filtration.

ADJUSTING FILTER PACK WHEN PRINTING FROM COLOUR NEGATIVES

If a test or print is too:	Subtract or	Add
Yellow	Magenta + Cyan (blue)	Yellow
Magenta	Cyan + Yellow (green)	Magenta
Cyan	Yellow + Magenta (red)	Cyan
Blue	Yellow	Magenta + Cyan (blue)
Green	Magenta	Cyan + Yellow (green)
Red	Cyan	Yellow + Magenta (red)

Illumination for viewing

The recommendation to examine your colour tests or prints in daylight is very often difficult to observe, because much of your printing may be done during the evenings and in the winter time. However, it will certainly be well worth your while putting a colour matching fluorescent light in a room where you can go to evaluate the test strips and prints you make. If you merely depend upon ordinary household lighting from tungsten lamps, you will often get an unpleasant shock when you come to look at your prints again in the morning. For example, it is particularly difficult to judge the true yellow content of a print under tungsten lighting.

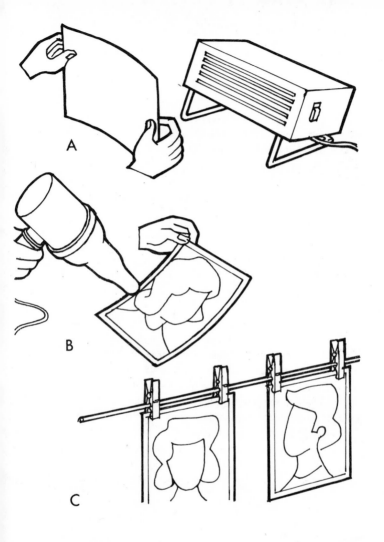

Neither resin coated colour papers nor Cibachrome print material can be dried by glazing. Alternative methods requiring no special equipment are: A – to hold the wet print in the current of air from a domestic fan heater, or B – to use an ordinary hair drier, or C – to hang the wet prints on a line with plastic pegs.

Wet or dry prints

While your tests are still a long way from being in balance it is not really necessary to dry them at the end of processing. If the print is merely rinsed for a minute or so following the bleach-fix treatment, it will be possible to assess it sufficiently well to decide on the correction required before the next exposure. But as the results become correct for density and more nearly correct for colour balance, it will be important to dry each test print before evaluating it. This is particularly true of Kodak colour papers because they incorporate couplers in a form which gives a print a bluish opalescent appearance until it is dry. Fortunately, resin coated papers can be dried quite quickly with a hot air drier of some kind.

Importance of consistent print processing

As you come nearer to the exposure and filtration required to produce a correctly balanced print from your reference negative you will also come to realise how dependent you are on consistent print processing. It is not much good deciding upon a final adjustment of 05 M to your filter pack if your next processing run suffers from some deviation in time or temperature. Quite small variations can be enough to more than offset such a change in filtration.

Be very careful to establish a strict routine for your processing cycle. It is not so much that you must develop for precisely three minutes rather than three minutes five seconds, but that it should always be either three minutes or three minutes five seconds. In the same way don't cut corners when rinsing or washing between stages – always do the same thing in the same way for the same time.

Colour
Papers

You do not have to understand much about colour papers in order to use them, any more than you need to know about its engine before you drive a car. But if you have some idea how colour paper works, you will be more likely to understand the reasons for any problems you may meet.

Basic construction

All colour papers are integral tripacks, put together in much the same way as colour negative and colour transparency films. In other words, three emulsion layers are coated in superimposition onto a paper base; one layer being sensitive to blue light, one to green light and the third to red. Nowadays both sides of the paper base are usually protected by very thin layers of polyethylene to prevent the absorption of processing liquids. The three emulsion layers and any separating layers are largely composed of gelatine. Of course the emulsion layers also contain silver halides and the necessary colour couplers.

Coating precision

It is very much more difficult to manufacture colour paper than it is to make black and white bromide paper. There are several reasons for the increased difficulty, but principally it is because of the extreme coating accuracy required. You can image just how precisely the thickness of each emulsion must be controlled if you remember that the total thickness of the three layers is only about one thousandth of an inch, and if any one of the three varies by as little as 5% or the equivalent of 15 millionths of an inch, it will cause a shift in the colour balance of the paper. If this were to occur within a sheet, it would make the paper totally useless.

Few manufacturers

Only relatively few manufacturers make colour papers – two in the U.S., one in the U.K., one in France, one in Germany and three in

Japan. There may be one or two smaller producers in Eastern Europe, but their papers are not usually available in the West. The silver dye bleach colour print material made in Switzerland and called Cibachrome is intended for printing directly from slides. The process is described separately on p. 158–163.

Just as with colour film products, there are two basic methods of ensuring that the couplers used in the emulsions coated on colour papers stay in their respective layers and do not diffuse out of them during processing. Kodak disperse their couplers in minute water permeable but water insoluble globules of a resinous plastic substance, while Agfa use colour couplers of such large molecular size as to literally entangle themselves in the structure of the gelatine of the emulsion with which they are mixed and coated.

Characteristic differences between colour development papers

These two solutions to the problem characterise all currently available colour development papers so that each type can be considered to be similar to either Ektacolor or Agfacolor paper. It is characteristic of the Kodak type of paper that because of the resin-like particles containing the dyes, a slight bluish opalescent appearance persists until prints are fully dried.

Having divided colour papers into two broad groups, it must be pointed out that it does not follow that all papers in one group will have the same speed, require the same processing or be capable of yielding the same results.

Resin-coated paper base

Until a few years ago, almost all colour and black and white papers for printing from negatives used an unprotected paper base support, so that most of the take-up of developer and other processing solutions was due to the paper base rather than the emulsion layers. This meant that a considerable amount of washing was necessary to avoid contamination between solutions and to ensure that finished prints did not deteriorate on keeping.

R.C. and P.E. papers

In America, and to a large extent in the U.K., the term 'resin-coated' has been abbreviated into R.C., while in Europe, Agfa-Gevaert decided to describe their papers as being polyethylene or P.E. coated. These two terms amount to the same thing.

Contrast grades

Black and white printing papers are usually made in four or five contrast grades, but most manufacturers supply their colour paper only in one grade. Although there are some differences in contrast between the papers of different manufacturers. The fact that (in most cases) one contrast grade is adequate, depends very largely upon uniform manufacture and processing of colour negative materials.

Surfaces

The surface texture of resin-coated papers is determined by the surface of the underlying resin layer itself. In other words, if the resin layer is left with the smooth surface it has after being applied to the paper base, then any emulsion layers coated on it will dry with a correspondingly smooth or glossy surface. If on the other hand the resin layer is embossed with some regular or irregular texture before emulsions are coated on it, then finished prints made on it will have a correspondingly semi-matt, or silk surface or finish.

Do not glaze

Resin-coated papers cannot be glazed by hot drying with emulsion in contact with a glazing plate or drum. If you think about it, you will see that the water contained in the emulsion layers after the final wash, would not be able to escape through the paper base because of the two protecting layers of polyethylene. Also, the polyethylene coat begins to soften at about 93°C; above which temperature, the prints are quickly ruined.

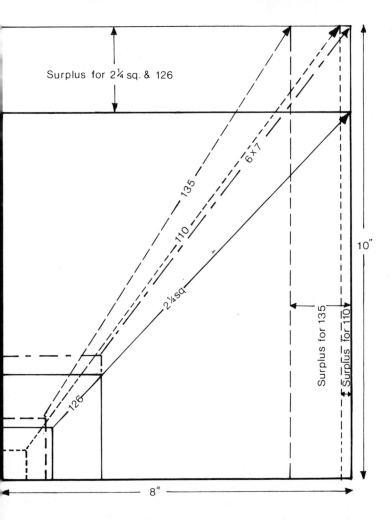

Surplus for 2¼ sq. & 126

135

6×7

110

2¼ sq

Surplus for 135

Surplus for 110

126

10"

8"

Because colour paper is expensive, it is necessary to consider ways of using it to best advantage. Unfortunately, an 8 × 10 inch sheet, while one of the more easily obtainable sizes, does not suit most negative formats. When enlarged to fit the smaller dimension, both 6 cm square and 126 Instamatic negatives result in a 2 × 8 inch surplus. If a 35 mm negative is enlarged to fit the 10 inch dimension, a surplus of nearly 1½ × 10 inches results. When enlarging a 6 × 7 cm or a 110 negative to 8 × 10 inches, practically nothing is wasted.

81

Ektacolor 37 R.C. Papers

Kodak makes a range of resin-coated colour papers with three different surface textures — glossy (F), smooth lustre (M) and silk (Y). Photofinishers have recently started making most of their prints on silk finish papers, although some still offer glossy prints as an alternative. The dyes found in the emulsion layers of Ektacolor 37 papers are much more stable and light-fast than they were in the early days of colour printing.

The chemistry that goes with Ektacolor paper is known as Ektaprint 3 — a three-bath process.

Agfacolor paper — MCN 310 Type 4

Agfa-Gevaert's polyethylene coated colour papers are known as Type 4 and their surface characteristics are coded as MCN 310 (glossy) MCN 312 (matt) and MCN 317 (silk). These papers can be processed in either of two chemistries — the four-bath Universal process or the three-bath process 85. It is the latter which the amateur is more likely to use because of its greater simplicity and shorter times.

Agfa describe their Type 4 papers as being "coated on a P.E. emulsion support" and say that "magenta dye contains very little blue and is therefore highly suitable for rendering flesh tones". Type 4 papers are also "very fast to light".

Batch to batch variations

For the reasons touched upon early on in the chapter, it is practically impossible for any manufacturer to produce batches of colour paper that do not differ slightly in colour balance. Differences within a batch will however be very small since colour paper is often used in one or even two thousand feet rolls for photofinishing, and in such applications it would be useless for the paper to vary from end to end of the same roll.

Value of single batch

It is always a problem for the amateur to decide what size and quantity colour paper he should buy. After all, it is rather expensive and a

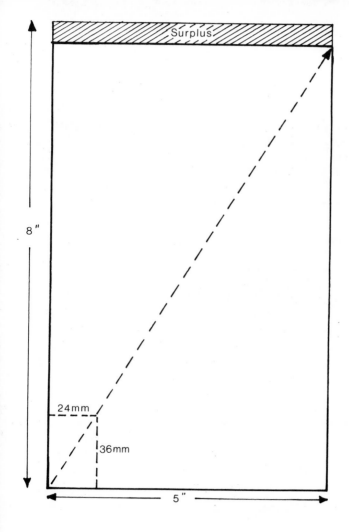

Surplus

8"

24mm

36mm

5"

If an 8 × 10 inch sheet is cut into two, the 5 × 8 inch pieces that result almost exactly suit an enlargement from the whole of a 35 mm negative.

significant proportion of it goes on test strips and prints that are not quite right. Nevertheless it will prove false economy if you buy as little paper as possible each time. Quite apart from the risk of running out just at the wrong moment, you are changing batches too frequently; and probably causing yourself a lot of unnecessary trouble and delay. It is true that the manufacturer always gives you some indication of the relative sensitivities of the three layers of each different batch of paper – usually indicated in filter values. However, even when you have done the necessary arithmetic to arrive at a new filter pack, you will be very lucky if you find you can change from one batch of paper to another without a hitch. So buy as much paper of one batch as you can afford.

Paper sizes

There are some rather good reasons why you may be well advised to settle on 8 in × 10 in as the standard size of paper you use. For one thing, this is very likely to be stocked by your dealer. Secondly, much of the equipment designed for colour printing is based on 8 in × 10 in as the standard size – print drums and special enlarger boards for example. Also, you can print an 8 in × 10 in sheet in a number of useful ways. You can use a single 8 in × 10 in sheet to contact print the whole of a 36 exposure 135 film or the 8, 10, 12 or 16 exposures on a 120 film. You can get four useful sized test prints on one sheet of paper or you can make four 4 in × 5 in prints of the same negative. It is true that neither 4 in × 5 in nor 8 in × 10 in are good formats on which to print 35 mm negatives or transparencies, but if the 8 in × 10 in is divided into two 8 in × 5 in pieces, then the whole of a 35 mm frame can be printed with only a small waste of paper.

Storage of paper

All sensitised photographic materials deteriorate more rapidly at high temperatures. In general, the emulsion layers become foggy and their speed and contrast change. It is necessary therefore to store a complex and expensive material like colour paper under conditions that will delay or even prevent such changes – in other words in a refrigerator or freezer.

Warm up period

When you take a box or packet of paper from cold storage, give it an hour or two to reach something like room temperature before removing the inner foil wrapping to take out the number of sheets you need at the time. If you don't leave this period for the paper to warm up, you may one day find that moisture forms on the surface of the sheets because they are cold enough to cause condensation.

Safelighting

Very little will be said about handling colour paper under a safelight. This is because when you are turning on the white light or moving into a lamplit room every four minutes to process a print in a light tight drum, you are in the dark for such relatively short periods, that you might just as well learn to work in complete darkness. To benefit at all from the low level of safelight offered by either Kodak's or Agfa's recommendations, it would be necessary to wait some five or ten minutes before you could expect to become dark adapted.

However, for those who would still like to try for themselves, these are the conditions the manufacturers specify:

Ektacolor 37 RC paper may be handled for a *limited period only* under the light from a 25 watt safe lamp fitted with a Kodak Safelight Filter No. 10 H (dark amber) or a 15 watt safelamp fitted with a Kodak Safelight Filter No. 13 (dark amber). Any paper must be kept at least four feet from the lamp.

Agfacolor papers can be handled for *not more than ten minutes* if kept at least 30 in away from the light from a 15 watt lamp behind an Agfa safelight screen No. 08.

Safelight fog

Safelight fogging of colour paper usually manifests itself in the form of lowered contrast and/or a bluish-green fog – over the image area *and* the borders of a print.

Colour
Paper
Processing

Print developing drums and greatly simplified processing sequences have made colour print processing very easy for the amateur – provided always that he will take care to be absolutely consistent in his chosen procedure.

Processing in dishes

Colour prints can be processed quite successfully in dishes, but there is little doubt that the job is simpler and more economical for the amateur who uses one or other of the several light-tight cylindrical print tanks that are now available.

It would be an over-simplification to say that the only critical step in processing a colour print is the development stage, but it is a fact that if this first step is carried out reproducibly and contamination of the developer is carefully avoided, then controlling the remaining steps should prove relatively easy.

Two basic chemistries

Just as there are two major types of colour paper – Ektacolor and Agfacolor – there are two basic chemistries for them: Ektaprint 3 and Agfa Process 85. In the U.S. these are often referred to as Type A and Type B chemistries. Because colour chemicals tend to be expensive, there is often a temptation to economise in some way, either by using substitute chemistry offered at a lower price or by using less than the manufacturer's indicated volumes or perhaps using a given volume of solution to process more prints than recommended. The motives for following any of these courses are quite understandable, and might even prove economical and successful, but while you are at the learning stage when unexplained difficulties are most likely to occur, do not risk confusing yourself by rejecting manufacturers' advice. Later, perhaps – but not while you have so much to learn.

In their continuous attempts to simplify and shorten processing procedures, Agfa and several independent chemical manufacturers offer processes which operate at very high temperatures. These high temperatures are not too difficult for a professional laboratory to achieve and maintain, but the amateur tends to be in difficulties when he tries to work with solution temperatures that are much above the ambient temperature of his workroom.

Fortunately, by using a print drum and one or other of the recommended procedures, it is now possible to maintain adequate control of processing temperature without the necessity for thermostatic equipment.

Preparation of solutions

The components making up the working solutions required for colour print processing are now often supplied as concentrated liquids and consequently they only need to be diluted to the final volume and brought to the required temperature before they are ready for use.

Three step colour print chemistry involves: development, a combined bleach-fix and a final stabilising treatment. Of these three steps, development is the one that must be controlled most carefully in terms of: 1, solution activity; 2, solution temperature: 3, time of treatment; 4, degree of agitation. Each of these factors will be considered later.

Ektaprint 3

Kodak Ektaprint 3 chemicals are supplied as two separate packages – Unit 1 containing the three part developer concentrates and Unit 2 including two part bleach-fix concentrates and a one part stabiliser. All these concentrates are used to make 1 litre each of the three working solutions.

Avoid contamination

The most important thing to remember when preparing the working solutions is to avoid all risk of contaminating the developer with any of the other solutions. You will be more likely to succeed in this if you use a separate measuring and mixing vessel for the developer and never use it for anything else. Now that plastic containers are so readily available, this is not an extravagance. Especially when you remember the cost of the paper and chemicals; and the time you would waste if your developer does not behave properly because of some unsuspected contamination with a trace of bleach-fix or some other solution.

Glass, stainless steel or rigid plastic containers can all serve for the mixing operations and either glass or plastic bottles can be used to store the working strength solutions. A dark or opaque bottle is recommended for storing the developer, but if you haven't a suitable bottle to hand, just make sure that you keep the developer out of bright daylight.

If you are not expecting to use most of the mixed developer within a few days, it is preferable to dispense the total volume into two or three smaller bottles, so that those not in use can remain full and stoppered to exclude air.

Mixing instructions

It is hardly necessary here to provide step by step mixing instructions for Ektaprint 3 chemistry, since an up to date instruction leaflet will be found in each Unit 1 package. This leaflet also gives details of the storage life of the three working solutions and from this table you will see that the developer will keep for rather less time than either the bleach-fix or the stabiliser.

Capacities of solutions

You will also notice that with Ektaprint 3, you can get almost three times more work out of the bleach-fix and stabilising solutions than you can from the developer. This is why you can buy Unit 1 kits separately from Unit 2. You may well find that you will form the habit of ordering three Unit 1 kits together with only one Unit 2 kit, so that the capacities of all three solutions work out at about the same.

Economy of solutions

While there is everything to be said for using a minimum quantity of developer and discarding it immediately after use, there is no reason why the same volumes of bleach-fix and stabiliser should not be used three times before you throw them away. Certainly I have been working in this way for some time now.

Divided kits

There is one other advantage of using liquid concentrates rather than powdered chemicals – you can, if you really want to, divide the several components of a kit into two halves, simply by carefully measuring out half the initial volumes, and retaining the other halves for future use. Dividing kits is not at all easy or even advisable with dry chemicals.

Ektaprint 3 procedure

There is nothing magic about a particular developing time and temperature combination, since within reasonable limits times can be increased and temperatures lowered – or vice versa – to give the same results. However, the steps recommended by Kodak for processing Ektacolor 37 RC paper in Ektaprint 3 chemistry are so simple and easy to remember for a temperature of 31°C (88°F) that there would seem to be little reason for wanting to change things.

PROCESSING STEPS FOR KODAK EKTACOLOR 37 RC PAPER IN EKTAPRINT 3 CHEMISTRY

Step	Time (minutes)	Temperature °C	°F
1. Developer. Begin timing as soon as the paper is wet with Developer.	3 ½	31	88
2. Bleach-Fix	1 ½	31	88
3. Wash	2	31	88
4. Stabilizer	1	31	88

Agfacolor 85 kit

Agfa-Gevaert, who have always been ready to supply small scale users with the necessary materials for colour printing, now offer a 1 litre — four bath — kit of chemicals (P85) for use with their polyethylene coated (Type 4) colour papers.

Unlike Kodak, who supply their colour processing chemicals in concentrated liquid form, Agfa uses powdered chemicals for the P85 kit. While most people consider that liquid concentrates make the job of solution preparation much easier, it is a fact that dry chemicals are generally more stable in their keeping properties than solutions, and therefore there is perhaps less risk of kits deteriorating after having been stored for a long time by either the customer or the photodealer. Just how important such considerations are, is a matter of opinion, but it does seem probable that all manufacturers will eventually supply their chemicals in liquid form because of the greater convenience that results.

Mixing instructions

There is no reason to describe detailed mixing procedures here, since every Agfacolor 85 kit contains an adequate instruction leaflet. However it may be worth noting that the first two components of the developer CD-A1 and A2, do not dissolve fully until a third component — CD-B — is added. Both the bleach-fix and the final bath (stabiliser) consist of two powder components, but the final bath also requires the addition of 5 ml of 30% formalin. The stop-bath is made up from only one powder.

Process 85

Agfacolor P.E. or resin coated papers, like other papers, can be safely processed at any temperature within a range such as 20°C to 30°C or between 68°F and 86°F. Agfa gives times for one-shot or total-loss processing in a drum at 20°C, 25°C and 30°C. Since even at the highest of these temperatures the processing sequence takes slightly

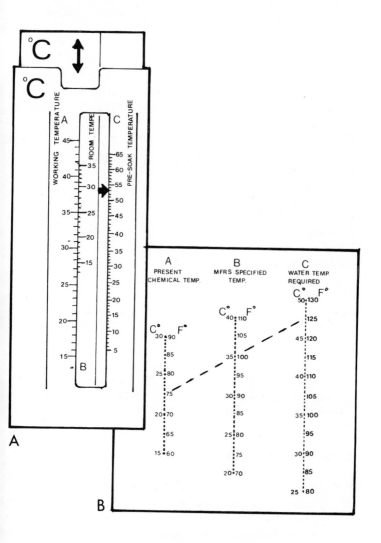

Either a sliding calculator of the kind supplied by Paterson — A, or a nomograph chart — B, such as included with many processing drums, will make it easy to determine the temperature required for the water you will use for pre-soaking and washing the prints you process.

longer than Ektaprint 3 – used at 31°C – I think most amateurs will choose to use P85 at 30°C (86°F).

By comparing the sequence of steps required for P85 with those used for Ektaprint 3, it will be seen that although P85 development requires only $2\frac{1}{4}$ minutes as compared with $3\frac{1}{2}$ minutes for Ektaprint 3, stop bath and rinse steps add an extra minute to the total time required for the Agfa process. Note that at 30°C, the developer is diluted in the ratio of 2 parts developer to 1 part water.

ONE-SHOT PROCESSING OF AGFACOLOR PAPER

Processing step	Time (mins) for processing at:		
	20°C (68°F)	25°C (77°F)	30°C (86°F)*
Developer	6	4	$2\frac{3}{4}$
Stop-Bath	$\frac{3}{4}$		$\frac{1}{2}$
(3% Acetic Acid)†	1		
Rinse	1	$\frac{3}{4}$	$\frac{1}{2}$
Bleach-Fix	4	3	2
Wash	4	3	2
Stabiliser	1	1	1

Notes:

* When processing at 30°C (86°F) the developer is diluted in the proportion of 2 parts of developer to 1 part of water (40 ml developer + 20 ml water).

† Acetic Acid must be obtained separately and a 3% solution prepared and used as Stop-Bath. This solutions keeps indefinitely.

The Simmard Color Drum

The Simmard tank was the first of its kind and remains one of the best of the small cylindrical print processors. The distinctive – and patented – feature of the Simmard drum is the eccentricity of its two end flanges – designed to give a slight rocking movement while the drum is rolled back and forth on a flat bench top. The importance of this device lies in the fact that a small volume of solution in the tank not only rotates concentrically with the drum, but is also urged from end to end parallel to the axis of the drum. This multi-directional flow

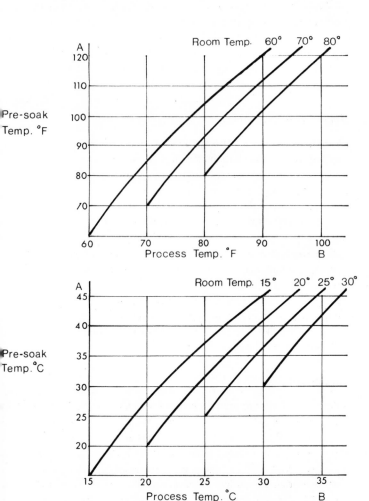

These two charts — one for Farenheit and the other for Centigrade — provide a ready means of determining the temperature of the pre-soak water you should use before processing a print in a Durst Codrum, when you already know the temperature in your work-room. The pre-soak temperature required for other kinds of processing drum might be slightly different, but this is still not so important as strict consistency.

of solution over the surface of the print ensures very efficient agitation, with no risk of streaks resulting from unidirectional flow.

The inside surface of the 8 in × 10 in Simmard drum has a number of slightly raised ribs which allow free access of solutions and wash water behind the print. This means that there is little risk of stains forming on the backs of prints.

Removable separators

During 1974, some changes were made in the design of the separators that slide into the inside of Simmard drums. Earlier models had two internally moulded ribs running from end to end of the drum, and when standing horizontally on a flat surface, these two walls formed a shallow trough into which each successive processing solution entered before coming into contact with the exposed paper as soon as the drum was rolled to and fro. It seems that under certain conditions and with some processes, unevenness could result from the slight shielding effect of the ribs – the trouble usually occurring at the edges of the print.

Simmard solved this problem by using round rod-like paper guides which ensure that solutions easily reach the edges of the paper. These 'Cling-Flow' guides are still easily removable and can be washed and dried between processes.

Larger drums

Two larger Simmard print tanks are available – one for 11 in × 14 in and another for 16 in × 20 in prints. The first of these will also take two 8 in × 10 in, four 5 in × 7 in, or six 4 in × 5 in; while the largest drum will accommodate a single 16 in × 20 in print or an 11 in × 14 in, or four 8 in × 10 in, eight 5 in × 7 in, or eight 4 in × 5 in.

The quantities of solution recommended for use in these two drums are: 150 ml (5 oz) for the 11 in × 14 in and 250 ml (8 oz) for the 16 in × 20 in.

Temperature control with Simmard Drum

Besides introducing their 'wave-wash' form of agitation, Simmard also decided to tackle the problem of solution temperature control

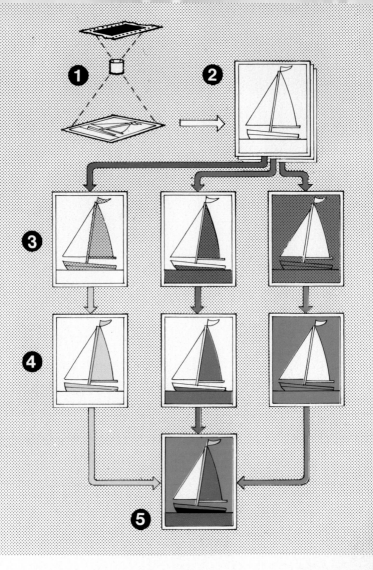

Printing from a colour negative: 1, An enlarged image of the colour negative is projected onto a sheet of colour paper. 2, By means of this single exposure, latent images are formed in the three emulsion layers of the colour paper. 3, The exposed print is then developed in a colour developing solution which forms three combined silver-plus-dye images; one dye is yellow, one magenta and the third cyan. 4, The silver that accompanies these images is then removed in a bleach-fix solution. 5, The three remaining dye images in superimposition on the same support form the finished colour print.

All 36 exposures of a 35 mm film can be contact printed on to an 8 x 10 in sheet of colour paper. If you use your enlarger as the light source for exposing the contact print, the filtration required for the proof sheet also serves as a useful guide for subsequent enlargements.

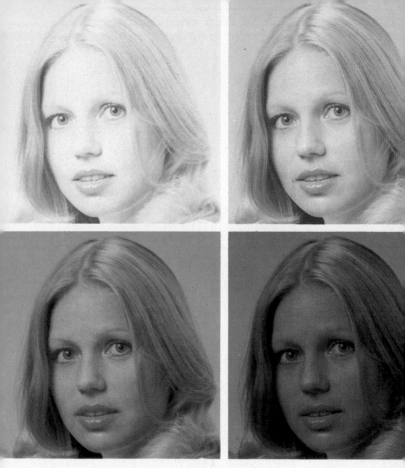

These four tests were expected to "straddle" the correct exposure for the particular negative. The four exposure times given were 5, 10, 20 and 40 sec and the filtration was 120Y and 80M. From these tests it was estimated that a 13 sec exposure would give the correct density.

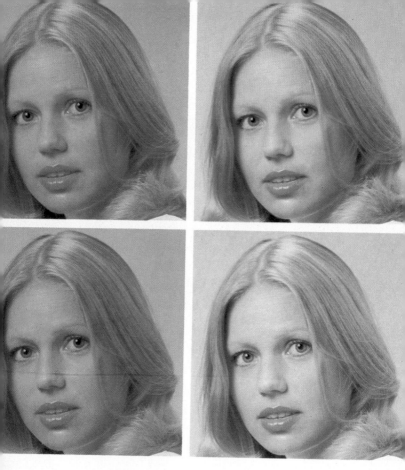

A colour test was then made, using these filters:
100Y and 50M *(top left)*; 100Y and 70M *(top right)*; 80Y and 70M *(bottom left)*; 110Y and 80M *(bottom right)*. All four exposures were for 13 sec.

EXPOSURE

40R

20R

×4

10R

×2

40M

20M

10M

NORMAL

10B

÷2

40B

20B

UNDER
EXPOSURE   ÷4

40Y

20Y

10Y

10G

20G

40G

10C

20C

40C

Ring-around for negative-positive printing.

By comparing your 'off-balance' tests or prints with this 'ring-around', you can decide more quickly what changes in exposure and/or filtration you need to produce a better result. Remember that when you have matched your tests with one of the pictures, you should then *add* the filter value that is indicated.

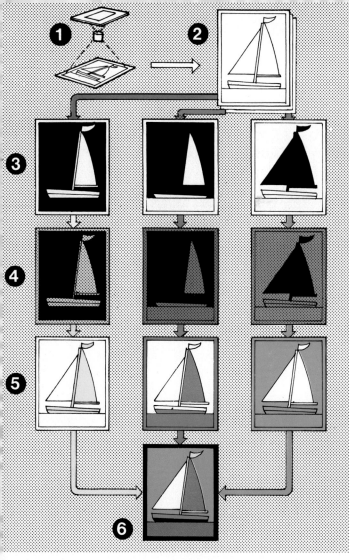

Reversal printing on Ektachrome RC paper. 1, An enlarged colour transparency image is projected on to reversal colour paper. 2, Three latent images are formed in the three emulsion layers. 3, These are first developed in a black and white developer, giving a silver image for blue, green and red components in the original. 4, Remaining unexposed parts are fogged. Colour development produces three silver and dye positive images, top layer, yellow, middle layer, magenta, and bottom layer cyan. 5, Bleaching and fixing removes unwanted silver, leaving only the dye images in the finished print, 6.

Opposite. The upper pair of prints illustrate a difference in colour balance that can result from having negatives on the same batch of film developed by two different laboratories. The prints were made under identical conditions. The lower pair of prints were made from two different batches of film and processed at the same time by the same laboratory. All the negatives were exposed identically.

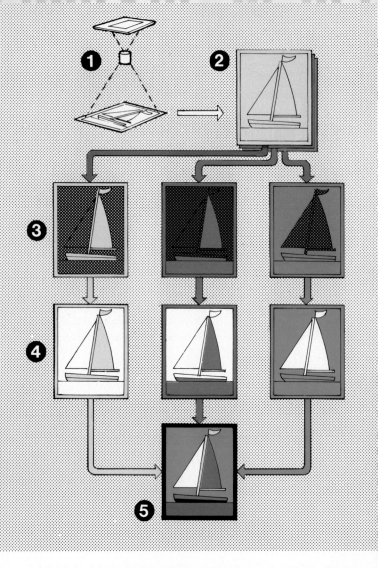

1, Enlarged colour transparency image is projected on to Cibachrome print material. 2, Three latent images are formed in the respective layers of the print material; each layer already contains a yellow, a magenta or cyan dye. 3, Black and white development gives three superimposed negative silver images—one each representing blue, green and red in the original. 4, The silver images and surrounding dye are removed in a special silver/dye bleach. 5, Superimposed yellow, magenta and cyan dye images remain in the finished print.

Twenty mounted 35 mm colour transparencies can be proof-printed on a sheet of 8 x 10 in colour paper.

Four test prints designed to embrace the correct exposure for a transparency. 10 secs was given for each test at: *top right* f5.6; *bottom right* f8; *top left* f11; *bottom left* f16. Filtration throughout was 30Y OM OC.

The best exposure was 10 secs at *f*11, but the colour balance was too yellow. Four more tests were therefore made using the following filtration: *top right* 20Y OM OC; *bottom right* OY 30M OC; *top left* 5Y OM 15C; *bottom left* OY OM 30C. The best result came from using 5Y +15C. The final print is reproduced on page 97.

UNDER
EXPOSURE

40C

20C

÷4

10C

÷2

40G

20G

10G

NORMAL

10Y

×2

20Y

40Y

OVER
EXPOSURE

×4

40B

20B

10B

10M   **20M**   **40M**

10R

20R

40R

Ring-around for reversal printing.
Equivalent exposure and filtration changes have less effect with reversal than neg.pos. printing. Colours follow filtration.

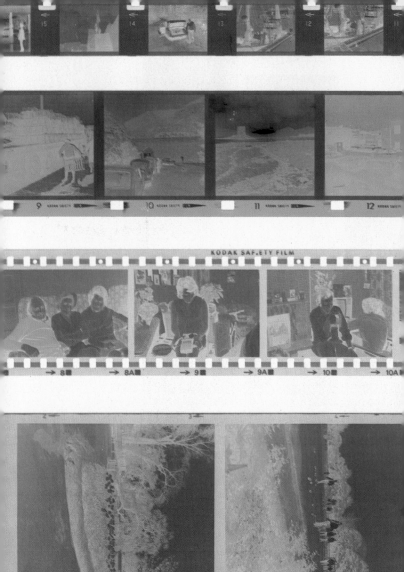

Some colour negative types and formats. *From top to bottom* 110 Kodacolor II, 126 Kodacolor X, 35 mm Kodacolor II, 120 (6 x 6 cm) Agfacolor CNS.

under the amateur's working conditions. In effect they said "never mind what your room temperature is, provided you know what it is and it is not likely to change quickly, and provided you also know the working temperature recommended for your particular type of colour paper and its chemistry". Knowing these two facts, you can then pre-heat the Simmard drum by filling it with water at such a temperature as will allow the tank, after being emptied, to give up just the right amount of heat to raise (or lower) the temperature of the small volumes of solution that you will use in the drum.

The correct temperature for the pre-heating water can easily be found from a nomograph supplied by Simmard. As an example, which could be typical of many work rooms in the U.K. during the winter months, let us assume an ambient temperature of about 63°F and a required working solution temperature of 88°F (Ektaprint 3). Then the pre-heat water would need to be at 104°F.

There is no reason why this pre-heat technique cannot be used with other types of print processing drums and in fact Agfa now provide charts calibrated in Fahrenheit and Centigrade, which will show you the temperature you should use for your pre-heat water when using the Durst Codrum.

Patterson Drum

The Patterson Colour Print Processor is different from other drums in that it is supplied with a supporting cradle and a handle that allows the drum to be rotated manually and slid from end to end throughout the processing cycle. Patterson have also devised a neat slide rule calculator for determining the required temperature of the pre-soak water.

Durst Codrum

The print processing drum sold by Durst is rather like the Simmard drum in that it incorporates a 'cam' action movement of solutions to ensure lateral as well as rotary flow. One end of the Codrum is at-tached to a flange in an eccentric manner, so that when the drum is rolled on a flat surface it rocks as it rolls. The Codrum has a completely smooth inner surface with none of the guides or raised ribs that are used in the Simmard tank. This means that greater care must be taken to locate prints in the Codrum so that they slide squarely into position without overlap or protrusion. Furthermore, because there are no ribs on the inner surface, the Codrum must always be scrupulously dried out before the next print can be slid into position, whereas, with the Simmard drum there is, in my experience, no necessity to be so very particular about drying the drum perfectly between prints.

The Durst Codrum provides the facility to pour a solution into its end cap and yet defer the commencement of processing until the drum is moved to the horizontal position and then rolled to and fro.

Kodak Printank

In 1973, Kodak introduced a colour processing drum in the U.K. and called it the Printank. This tank is made of grey plastic material and has a lid sealing one end of the drum by means of a very tight fitting rubber 'O' ring. This lid fits so tightly on some tanks that it is difficult to believe that it has to be removed and replaced every time a print is processed. The lid also supports a central filling tube into which the processing solutions are poured and which conducts these solutions to the bottom of the drum where they cannot touch the print until the tank is moved into a horizontal position. There is a cap to cover the filling hole at one end of the tank and another, corresponding cap for draining from the other end. There are feet moulded into the base of the tank so that it will stand vertically while solutions are poured in.

Temperature control with the Printank

Unlike Simmard, Kodak recommend floating the loaded Printank on the surface of a sink or bowl of water maintained at 32°C, so as to provide a working temperature of 31°C inside the drum – 31°C being the preferred temperature for Ektaprint 3 chemistry.

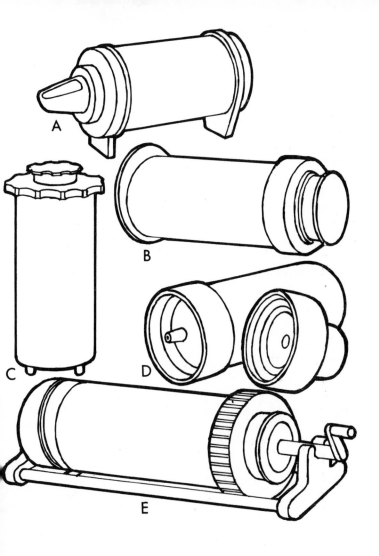

There are several different types of print processing drum, among them A – the Simma-color (Besseler), B – the Durst Codrum, C – the Kodak Printank, D – the Cibachrome (U.S.) drum, and E, – the Paterson Color print Processor.

Other print processing drums

There is another kind of print drum made in the U.S. and sold with the Cibachrome processing kit. The feature of this type of drum is that developer can be poured into one end while the tank is held vertically, and then, after development has proceeded while the drum is rolled to and fro, in a horizontal plane, the tank is again upended so that the developer is discarded from the lower end while the next solution is poured into the top. These simultaneous draining and filling operations certainly save time and the fact that each solution is retained in the filler cap until the moment the drum is switched to the horizontal position means that processing times can be very short and still be accurate – an important consideration when working at high temperatures.

Another advantage of this kind of double-ended tank is that simply by using a longer tube you can process larger prints.

Preparations for processing

Remembering that an exposed print must be loaded into your processing drum in complete darkness, you will do well to prepare things thoroughly before you finally switch off the room light. If you are using the Simmard procedure, you will have read the temperature in your working area – whether it be a darkroom, your bathroom or your kitchen, and then, knowing the processing temperature recommended for your colour paper and chemistry you will have found what temperature you need to have your reservoir – a plastic bucket will do – of tempered water.

Pour out the required amounts of developer, bleach-fix and stabilising solutions and make sure that you label or mark each beaker or container in some way that will ensure that they are invariably used for the same solution. Numbering them clearly – 1, 2 and 3 – should be sufficient. Then – and this in my experience is very important – put the beakers or measures in some place where they can be easily reached, but cannot easily be knocked over in the dark, particularly when you come to roll the drum to and fro on the bench top.

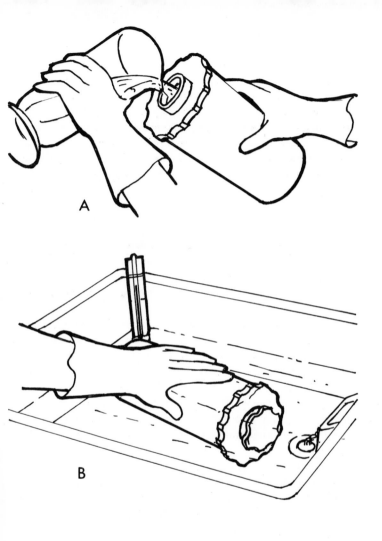

The Kodak Printank is light tight when its large knurled end cap is pressed into position. After developer has been poured in – A, and the smaller cap has been added, the tank becomes watertight, so that it can be floated in a water bath – B to maintain the required temperature during the development stage.

Practice in the light

Practice putting paper into your drum in white light before you attempt to do it with an exposed print in darkness. A little time spent on this will ensure that you don't run into difficulties and find yourself handling prints excessively with the consequent risk of marking them. Assuming you are working with a Simmard drum, when the exposed print, or prints, have been located properly, the cap of lid is placed firmly on the end of the drum, using the location pin as a guide. Then a light can be switched on or you can move into daylight.

Pre-soak

Next, stand the drum on end and fill it with water at the temperature you have determined from the nomograph or chart. This tempering water can be prepared beforehand in a half-filled plastic bucket, and the rest of this water will be used for rinsing and washing as required in the processing sequence.

Leave the pre-soak water in the drum for one minute; then pour it away, making sure that you shake out the last drops before laying the tank horizontally on its feet in a sink or on a work top. Then pour the previously dispensed 50 ml dose of developer into the spout of the drum. The temperature of the developer will be at the ambient temperature of your workroom. In other words, don't bring the bottle of stock developer into the room just before you need to use it, but make sure that it has had time to reach equilibrium with the surrounding temperature.

The developer you poured into the drum will have entered a trough formed by the two longitudinal separators inside the tank, so that development cannot commence until the drum is rolled, and the developer escapes into the tank proper, to flow over the surface of the exposed print.

Rolling the drum

So, when you are ready, start the timer and at the same time commence rolling the drum back and forth within the limits set by its

118

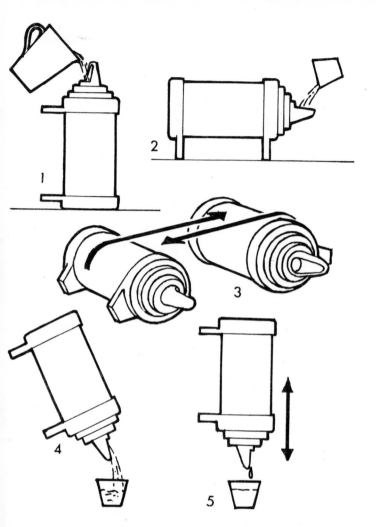

The principal stages involved when using a print processing drum, filling the tank (in this case a Simma-color drum) with pre-soak water at the required temperature (1), and after one minute emptying it before pouring in the measured quantity of developer (2). Then, having started the timer, the tank is rolled to and fro during the period of development (3). During the ten seconds before the end of development, all solution is poured out (4) and shaken from the tank (5).

protruding feet. The rate of to and fro movement should be about 2 or 3 seconds per cycle and it should be maintained throughout the processing period.

If you get tired or bored with this chore, you may decide to invest in an automatic agitator, which will roll your tank back and forth while still maintaining the wave-wash effect. But for a beginner, this is perhaps something of a luxury.

Stopping

Fifteen seconds before the end of whatever development time is required, pour away the developer, shaking all the drops out of the spout with the tank upended. Then, place the drum back on its feet and pour in either the stop-bath or the bleach-fix according to the process you are using. Again start the timer and again roll the tank. Don't delay at this point in the process, since the wet print will continue to develop in the meantime.

At the end of the stop or bleach-fix stage, the stop bath should be poured away, but the bleach-fix solution may be poured back into its own beaker for such further use as its working life allows – usually two or three prints at least. The next step will usually be a rinse or wash.

Rinsing and stabilising

The tempered water remaining in the bucket is suitable for washing or rinsing, since its higher temperature will tend to speed up the removal of residual chemicals from the print. You can either use a reasonably large volume – say 250 ml – for the required length of washing time, or several smaller volumes for a series of separate rinses. Probably the sequence of rinses is the more efficient way, although with resin-coated papers, thorough washing is no longer difficult to achieve.

The final processing treatment is usually in a stabilising solution, but this is not a critical part of the process.

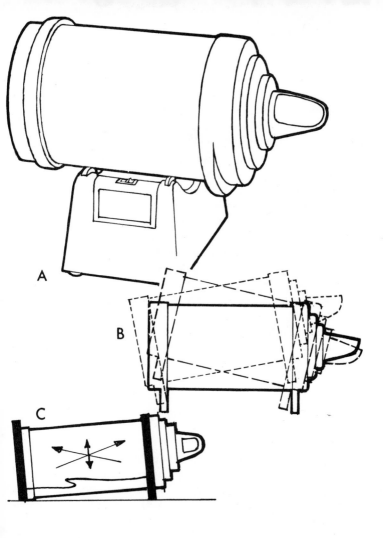

The Simma-roller-A, can be used to provide agitation automatically with any type of colour print processing drum. Eccentric rollers on the motor driven agitator tilt the drum from side to side – B, while it is being rotated. When a Simma-color drum is rolled to and fro by hand on a level surface, both lateral and rotary flow – C, is imparted to the solution in the drum.

Establish a routine

In so far as different tank manufacturers and different colour paper manufacturers recommend somewhat different requirements and methods for their tanks and papers, it is not necessary here to describe any particular procedure. But one point can usefully be made; whatever your choice of drum or paper, once you have established a satisfactory technique which produces good results – do not change it in any way unless you have some very good reason for doing so.

For instance, if you normally leave the pre-soak water in your drum for a minute then always make it one minute – not half a minute because you are in a hurry. Then when you drain out the pre-soak water, drain it all away – even shaking the tank to remove the last few drops. If you are careless about draining the tank completely at this stage, your developer becomes diluted slightly. A diluted developer will surely be that much less active than you expected. Again, when it comes to discarding developer, make sure that the time you take to do so is always the same – perhaps 15 seconds, to ensure that all developer really has been poured and shaken out of the drum. Similarly, when the bleach-fix solution is poured into the tank, be sure to start rolling the drum immediately in order to avoid streaking.

Importance of reproducibility

By carefully doing the same things in the same way each time, you will find that you are able to obtain quite reproducible results – a very important consideration when you are nearing final filtration for a print, perhaps involving the use of 05 filter adjustments – representing colour differences that could easily be offset by inconsistent processing.

Achieving
More Precise
Colour Balance

Those of you who by now have made a few colour prints will have come to realise that the most difficult part of the job is the determination of correct filtration and exposure for each different negative. Fortunately, once the correct conditions of exposure have been found for a representative negative from a single roll of film, it is quite likely that the other negatives on that roll will yield good results if you use the same filtration. You will still have to decide the correct amount of exposure to give each negative – something which takes a good deal more time than it does when you are making black and white prints and can judge a test strip within a minute or so while it is still in the developer dish.

Getting the density right

It is a good rule in colour printing to get the density of a print about right before worrying too much about its colour balance. While a print remains either too light or too dark, any changes you make to modify its colour will be much more difficult to assess than if the print is about right for density.

Contact printing

One of the simplest ways of getting some indication of the relative exposures required for a range of different negatives is to contact print them on the same sheet of paper. An 8 in × 10 in sheet of colour paper will allow you to proof print all the negatives on a 36 exposure roll of 35 mm film or a roll of 120 film.

Your earlier work will have taught you the correct conditions of exposure for your reference negative and if your next set of negatives was made on the same batch of colour negative material, and you continue to use the same batch of colour paper, then this same filtration should be used to expose your contact prints.

Contact proof printing

With nothing in the negative carrier, adjust the enlarger so as to produce an illuminated area on the easel slightly larger than the sheet

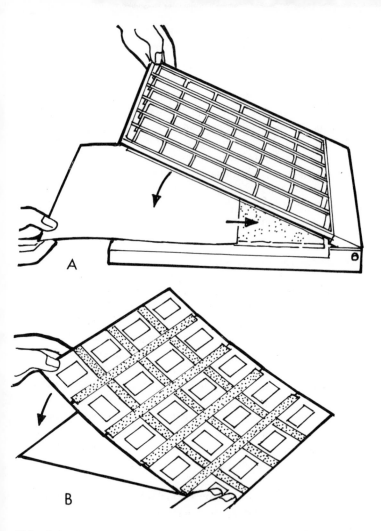

This printing frame – A, is designed for making contact prints from 35 mm – or 126 Instamatic – negatives onto a sheet of 8 × 10 in. paper. A thirty-six exposure length of 35 mm film is cut into six strips of six frames. When contact printing colour slides it is not necessary to remove them from their mounts, but it is useful to tape them together temporarily as in B. Like this they can be easily positioned on the sheet of printing paper. Twenty slides can be printed on one 8 × 10 in. sheet.

you are to expose – say a 9 in × 11 in area for 8 in × 10 in paper. Then stop down the lens to f8 and, with the contact frame in position complete with negatives and paper, give a trial exposure of 10 seconds. Use whatever filtration you had when you made the best print from your reference negative.

After processing the contact print sheet you may well find that exposure will need adjustment so that there are neither too many light nor too many dark frames in among the images. The overall colour balance should be reasonably good: if it is not, then something has changed since you made your best reference print. Don't be too worried if you have to adjust both colour and density, but if you find this part difficult – and you will not be alone if you do – then you should make yourself a set of ring-around prints.

Make your own ring-around

A ring-around series is simply a set of colour prints that have been carefully made to show the effects of uniform changes in colour filtration and exposure time. One might think of them as the scales you normally have to learn before you can properly play the piano or violin. Be assured that any time you spend in the preparation of a ring-around series will be well repaid by the greater confidence you will have when making subsequent filtration and exposure adjustments. You can refer to the ring-around reproduced in the colour section of this Photoguide as an indication of the various filtration and exposure changes you might use when exposing your own prints. As always, make sure your central reference print is as good as you can possibly make it before you ring the changes required for the comparison prints.

Mount the final set of prints on a single card for ease of reference and always refer to the prints under daylight or a colour matching fluorescent light.

First tests

A set of ring-around prints can only help you when you have already made a test strip or print and you need to know what changes to make before you make the next attempt. Before any of this can happen, you have had to decide what filtration and exposure you will give for your first test. As we have seen, there only needs to have been one significant change from the conditions you used for your optimum reference print, and you will again have to get back on target by using your own judgment.

What are these changes or differences that we must contend with? The more important of them are: 1, a different brand or type of colour negative film; 2, a change in negative processing conditions; 3, a different kind of colour paper; 4, a change in paper processing conditions; 5, a change in enlarging conditions.

Let us look at the significance of these factors one by one.

Different types of film

Between 1960 and 1970, Kodacolor X film processed in C22 chemistry became an almost universal amateur standard throughout most of the world. However, in 1971, with the advent of Pocket Instamatic cameras and the 110 size cartridge films to go in them, Kodak introduced a new — finer grained — colour negative material called Kodacolor II together with a new chemistry — C41. Kodacolor II is not just different by being finer grained, but it also has a mask that is lower in density and different in colour from the mask used in Kodacolor X.

As a result of these changes, the printing filtration required for a Kodacolor II negative is different from that needed for an equivalent negative made on Kodacolor X film.

Typically Kodacolor X negatives need about 50 Y and 40 M, whereas Kodacolor II need about 120 Y and 80 M.

In Europe and some other parts of the world, quite a lot of Agfacolor negatives are exposed by amateur photographers, and here again, there has been a succession of different Agfacolor films — all of which required their own special chemistry. The first Agfacolor negative film was unmasked, but in recent years Agfacolor has incorporated a mask, although it is not quite the same as Kodacolor X and certainly not the same as Kodacolor II.

Compatible colour negative films

Several film manufacturers like GAF and 3M in the United States and Fuji and Konishiroku (Sakura) in Japan, market films that are said to be comparable with either Kodacolor X or, more recently, Kodacolor II. This does not necessarily mean that if you expose a Kodak film alongside one of these compatible films then process them together in the approved Kodak chemistry that you will be able to print both negatives successfully at the same filtration or exposure. In fact it is almost certain that this will not be possible and you usually will find that you need to make some adjustment to ensure optimum results from these so-called compatible films.

Batch to batch film changes

The differences between batches of the same type of film are not usually very great — certainly not as large as they used to be. But we must remember that even slight changes in the relative speeds of the three emulsion layers can be enough to result in our needing a change in filtration that can only be determined by trial; whereas the same negatives, printed on an automatic integrating printer by a photofinisher, would certainly yield correctly balanced prints.

So whenever you can, buy the films you need in reasonably large quantities so as to ensure that you will be working with the same batch for as long a period as possible. Be sure, however, to store them in a refrigerator, otherwise they will slowly change.

Negative processing differences

This source of variation is difficult to avoid, and it is the more serious because of the many ways in which processing can depart from optimum conditions. Faulty development of a colour negative can alter the effective speed of the film, it can change its contrast, the mask density can vary, fog can be higher than it should be, or most serious the relative contrast of the three emulsion layers can change. When the last trouble occurs, there is practically nothing that can be done to correct the mistake at the printing stage.

Crossed contrasts can, for example, result in your print having magenta highlights and green shadows, and no amount of juggling with filters will eliminate these. The best you can ever do in these cases is to compromise between the colour of the lighter tones and that of the shadows according to the nature of the picture.

If, in order to guard against variations in negative processing, you decide to always do the job yourself, I can only commend your enthusiasm and impress upon you the need to establish a precise procedure and then stick to it meticulously. There is one thing I would warn you against. If at any time you are tempted to deal with a roll of negatives you know to be badly under or overexposed, by treating it in some non-standard way or by switching to a different developer – then don't. Almost certainly you will so upset the contrast balance between the three image layers as to make it impossible to get a good print.

Should you decide to get your negatives processed by a photofinisher or professional laboratory, you may have to shop around a bit before deciding who shall do your work regularly. By spending a little money on ordering prints at the time you send your film for development, you will at least quickly discover who is doing his job properly. If the prints he makes for you are not satisfactory, then it will not give you confidence to entrust your negative processing to him – even though it often can happen that bad prints are made from perfectly good negatives.

Different types of colour paper

From time to time, you may be tempted to desert whatever brand of colour paper you began to print with, in order to see whether you can get better results with some other kind of paper. If you do switch, then allow yourself some time to get the best possible print on the new paper using your reference negative. If after several attempts you are not satisfied with any of the results you get from this negative on the new paper, perhaps it is because the paper you were using was not so bad after all.

Batch to batch differences in colour paper

Here we have one of the more frequent causes of difficulty in colour printing. Just when you feel you have things under reasonable control and the next print will be perfect, you discover that the test you have just assessed was made on the last sheet of paper from the packet. Consider yourself lucky if you have some more paper from the same batch. If you have not, then you must sit down with pencil and paper, and use the information given on the old and new packets to work out the changes in filtration you will need to compensate for the differences in the relative red, green and blue sensitivities of the two different batches of paper.

This is how you do it. Note the filtration given on the packet or box of paper you have just used up, and subtract these values from the filter pack you have been using to print your reference negative and other similar negatives. Let's imagine that the filters you have been happily using were 50 Y and 30 M, while the batch rating given for the old paper was 10 Y and 10 M. Then your first sum would be:

$$
\begin{array}{r}
50\,\text{Y} \quad 30\,\text{M} \quad 0 \\
\text{subtract} \quad 10\,\text{Y} \quad 10\,\text{M} \\
\hline
40\,\text{Y} \quad 20\,\text{M}
\end{array}
$$

Then add to this result the filtration values given for the next batch of paper — say +20 Y and +10 M.

$$
\begin{array}{r}
40\,\text{Y and }20\,\text{M} \\
\text{add} \quad 20\,\text{Y and }10\,\text{M} \\
\hline
60\,\text{Y and }30\,\text{M}
\end{array}
$$

A possible new filter pack would then be 60 Y and 30 M. You will notice the word possible; it is practically impossible to forecast precisely the result of changing from one batch of colour paper to another. The best that can be done is to get fairly near to the new filtration and thereby reduce the number of tests you will have to make.

Before leaving this problem of trying to calculate the filter pack required for a new batch of paper we should look at two cases that are not quite so straightforward as the one given above.

Supposing the filter values given on the old packet of paper were negative in value – say −10 Y and −10 M. If we still assume that we had been using the same filter pack to obtain good prints from our reference negative, namely 50 Y and 30 M. Then how do we subtract −10 Y and −10 M from this? Well, we must remember that subtracting minus values is equivalent to adding. So, the result will be:

$$
\begin{array}{ll}
 & 50 \text{ Y and } \quad 30 \text{ M} \\
\text{minus} & -10 \text{ Y and } \times 10 \text{ M} \\
\hline
\text{result} & 60 \text{ Y and } 40 \text{ M}
\end{array}
$$

To which must be added the values of the new batch of paper given on the packet, and these we have supposed to be 20 Y and 10 M. So that the pack we should try in this case would be:

$$
\begin{array}{ll}
 & 60 \text{ Y and } 40 \text{ M} \\
\text{add} & 20 \text{ Y and } 10 \text{ M} \\
\hline
 & 80 \text{ Y and } 50 \text{ M}
\end{array}
$$

One other complication can arise if cyan filter values become involved, so that you might end up with a pack containing densities of all three subtractive colours – yellow, magenta and cyan. There is nothing wrong with such a combination of filters *except* that it wastes printing light. Inevitably some neutral grey density will be present in a pack comprising filters of all three colours. Although this will not affect colour balance one way or the other, it does cause a loss of light. To remove neutral density from the filter pack, you subtract an equal density of yellow, magenta and cyan from the pack. For example, suppose your calculations result in a pack comprising 80 Y, 50 M and 20 C. You can subtract 20 Y, 20 M and 20 C from this. So you actually use a pack comprising 60 Y and 30 M. There is never any need to use more than two primary colours in your filter pack.

Exposure adjustments

In colour printing, you cannot significantly change the colour – and therefore the density – of your filter pack without considering the influence such changes have on the exposure time you need for the next print. In the example we have used so far, the additional density of the pack amounts to only 10 Y which has so little effect on overall exposure that it can be disregarded.

However, when you change paper batches, these may also require different exposure times. Suppose the exposure rating given on the new packet or box of paper is 120, and that on the 'old' packet was 90. If the exposure you were using to obtain a good print from your reference negative onto the old batch of paper was 10 seconds, then the exposure you will probably need for the reference negative on the new paper will be 10 × 120/90 or 13½ seconds.

Changing filters means changing exposure

Pay close attention to the changes in exposure that must be made to compensate for almost any change you make to your filter pack. If you are careless about this do not be surprised if you end up with prints that are nicely balanced in colour, but are either a bit too light or a bit too dark.

The problem arises from a number of factors. First of all, colour negative printing papers have to be relatively high in contrast, and as a result they have little exposure latitude. This means that quite small changes in filtration (even the removal of an .05 filter from a pack) can have a noticeable effect on the density of the next print; unless you allow for it.

When a single filter is placed in the path of the printing light, you lose light firstly because the filter has two surfaces, and some light is reflected back from each of these surfaces and never reaches the negative, and secondly, because the filter is there to absorb light of one of the three primary colours. The amount of light lost by absorption naturally depends on the density of the filter. The exposure compensation you need to make also depend upon this and on the colour of the filter. A yellow filter (of a given density) has less visual effect upon a print than does a magenta filter (of the same density) which, in urn has slightly less effect than a cyan filter (again of the same density). The reasons are perhaps not too difficult to follow. There are separate yellow, magenta and cyan images of the same subject within a print. The cyan image contributes most to the overall density, followed by the magenta; and the yellow image makes a comparatively smaller contribution still.

Exposure Factors

If all correction filters of the same nominal rating really had the same density, only one set of filter factors or tables would be required, but since there are some differences according to manufacture, you should always refer to the factors provided by the maker of the filters you are using.

To change your exposure, first divide your original time by the factor for *each* filter you have taken from the pack. Then multiply it by the factor for each one you have added. For example, suppose you have removed a 20 M and added a 10 Y. The factors may be 1.3 for the 20 M and 1.1 for the 10 Y. If your original exposure was 26 seconds, then your new figure will be 26 × 1.1/1.3, or 22 seconds.

Alternatively, filter manufacturers supply sliding or rotating calculators to make the adjustment even easier. These are simply physical methods of operating the factors, just as a slide rule is a physical method of using logarithms.

TABLE OF FILTER FACTORS FOR KODAK COLOUR PRINTING FILTERS

Filter Value	Factor	Filter Value	Factor	Filter Value	Factor
025 Y	1.2	025 M	1.2	025 C-2	1.1
05 Y	1.2	05 M	1.3	05 C-2	1.2
10 Y	1.2	10 M	1.4	10 C-2	1.3
20 Y	1.2	20 M	1.5	20 C-2	1.5
30 Y	1.2	30 M	1.6	30 C-2	1.9
40 Y	1.3	40 M	1.7	40 C-2	2.1
50 Y	1.3	50 M	1.8	50 C-2	2.2

Note: Cyan −2 filters should be used for printing Ektacolor Papers because of their better absorption of the infra-red part of the spectrum.

TABLE OF FILTER FACTORS FOR AGFACOLOR PRINTING FILTERS

Filter Value	Factor	Filter Value	Factor	Filter Value	Factor
05 Y	1.1	05 M	1.2	05 C	1.1
10 Y	1.1	10 M	1.2	10 C	1.2
20 Y	1.2	20 M	1.2	20 C	1.3
30 Y	1.2	30 M	1.3	30 C	1.4
40 Y	1.2	40 M	1.4	40 C	1.5
50 Y	1.2	50 M	1.5	50 C	1.7
99 Y	1.4	99 M	2.0	99 C	2.5

To use these tables multiply old exposure time by factor if filter is added
divide exposure time by factor if filter is removed.

Fading of filters

A large proportion of your negatives can be printed easily once you
have established the filtration required for your particular printing
conditions. That is to say, for your enlarger, the type of film you use
and the batch of colour paper you have in stock. Most negatives will
need the same or similar filter packs. This may mean that you are
leaving a few of your filters in the enlarger all the while. Consequently
if you make a lot of prints, there is some risk of the central area of one
or more of the filters in the pack fading. Any such change is, of course
very gradual; but if undetected leads to confusion sooner or later. So
from time to time lay each of the filters from your colour pack on a
sheet of white paper and check whether there is any evidence of
fading. If there is, replace any faulty filters as soon as possible.

Importance of U.V. and Infra-red absorbing filters

The presence of both an ultra-violet and an infra-red (heat) absorbing
filter certainly helps to reduce the risk of your filters fading. But it is
in any case important to use these filters whenever they are specified
by a manufacturer of colour paper. The sensitivity of colour paper

usually extends some way into both the ultra-violet and the infra-red regions of the spectrum. To obtain clear cut records of blue, green and red light, it is then essential to eliminate any chance of recording unwanted ultra-violet or infra-red radiation. So if the paper manufacturer calls for an ultra-violet and an infra-red absorbing filter, it makes sense to use them if you want to get the best out of your colour paper.

Different enlarging conditions

If you always made enlargements of the same size, from the same negative format, if the lamp in your enlarger never burnt out and if the supply voltage to the lamp never varied, you could probably disregard your enlarger as a source of variation in colour printing. But in practice you will want to make large prints sometimes and small ones at other times, you will have to change a lamp from time to time and you will be very lucky indeed if your electricity supply does not drop by as much as 10 per cent below its normal rating at periods of peak demand.

All these variables can have an effect on the colour balance of your colour prints and when you are sometimes looking for an explanation for unexpected shifts in balance, you should consider these kinds of variables along with the other possible causes.

Reciprocity failure

Some colour papers suffer from what is known as reciprocity failure. Reciprocity failure is merely a way of describing the fact that a photographic material does not respond in a strictly proportional manner over wide differences in exposure time. In other words an exposure of 5 seconds at $f5.6$ might not give exactly the same result as one of 40 seconds at $f16$, even though everything else was *exactly* the same.

Colour papers vary in the way they follow or depart from the so called reciprocity law, but the best way of avoiding any difficulty from this cause is to keep your exposures as similar in time as possible. That is to say, stop down the enlarging lens to give reasonably long exposures – say 10–15 seconds – when making small enlargements and open up the lens to allow something like the same exposure time when making bigger enlargements or when printing from dense negatives. If you can manage to arrange for most of your exposures to fall somewhere between 10 seconds and 30 seconds you can forget about reciprocity failure.

Changing lamps

The colour of the light produced by an incandescent lamp with a tungsten filament varies slightly throughout its life and the variation is greatest during the first hour or so of use. So if you can, run your spare lamp for an hour or so before you have to take it into regular use to replace one that has burned out. A simple way to do this is to use your spare lamp for a black-and-white printing session before you need to change the old one. That way you have a 'run-in' bulb ready at any time.

Supply voltage

A difference of 10 volts or more in the supply to an enlarger lamp will produce quite perceptible changes in both density and balance of a colour print. Roughly, a 10 volt difference is equivalent to an 05 filter; more than 10 volts means a more significant change, even as much as a 10 filter.

In many areas in the winter time and at peak hours of consumption, a 20 volt difference on a nominal 240 volt supply, is not at all unusual. So if you do disregard this source of variation, you must not be surprised to get some unusual results from time to time.

Voltage adjustment

The cheapest way of dealing with this problem is to use an adjustable resistance or a variable transformer in circuit with a voltmeter, so the supply voltage can be checked and if necessary adjusted immediately

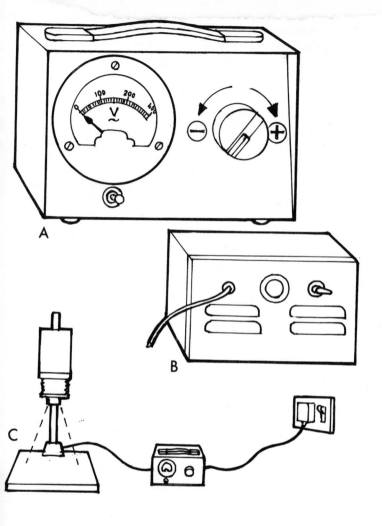

A voltmeter and a variable resistance – A, can be used to adjust the voltage supplied to your enlarger lamp, thereby ensuring constant light output. Although more expensive, a constant voltage transformer – B, will do the job automatically over a wide variation of input voltages. Whatever control device you choose, insert it between the mains supply and the enlarger as in C.

prior to making every exposure. Relatively simple and inexpensive units of this kind are made by Rayco. Naturally, with such a unit, you always run your lamp at a voltage slightly below the lowest dip you expect in the mains.

Constant voltage transformer

A fit and forget solution to the problem costs more, but can be achieved by using a constant voltage transformer, which will allow the supply voltage to vary by 20 volts on either side of the nominal rating while the output voltage for the circuit remains near enough constant.

There are some rather cheap electronic voltage controllers on the market that seem to work only if the current taken by the enlarging lamp exactly matches the rating of the controller – which is not always possible. If you should decide to buy one of these units at least check its performance with a voltmeter before relying on it.

Colour heads and dichroic filters

Filter fading can be completely eliminated by using what are known as interference filters. These are normally used only in colour heads (see p. 66).

Nearly all the colour heads on the market now depend upon non-fading interference filters and only the mechanical ways of adjusting the filters are different. The colour of the light entering the integrating chamber is adjusted either by moving more or less of the yellow, magenta and cyan transmitting dichroic filters into a concentrated part of the beam of light entering the integrating box; or by adding together suitable quantities of red, green and blue light from these filtered sources. Provided the mechanical means of adjusting the filters is well designed, it is possible to achieve an infinite number of different positions for the three filters, and furthermore, to reproduce these settings at any time.

For a while after their initial introduction, enlarger colour heads were too expensive for even the keen amateur to afford, but recently manufacturers such as Durst and Simmons have begun to produce colour enlargers and colour heads which will certainly be within the reach of some hobbyists.

The advantage that comes from using a colour head instead of a filter pack is not just confined to the elimination of fading. Convenience and accuracy both result from being able to choose from an infinite number of filter combinations merely by adjustment of the settings on three scales.

Because they are so different in principle and in the way they are used, it is not possible to equate directly the performance of these dichroic filters with any set of dyed filters. Consequently if you change over from using filter packs to using a dichroic colour head you will have to make some tests to reconcile the filter values you have been using with the scale values on your colour head.

Paper processing variations

Now that most amateurs are using drums and one shot chemistry to process their prints, the chances of variation occuring in print processing have been greatly reduced. Nevertheless, it is possible to inadvertently introduce some variable in your processing technique. Therefore it will pay you to make a number of identical exposures from your reference negative and to store these in your refrigerator so that you can take one out whenever you are experiencing unexplained variations in quality, and process it to see that your chemistry and your processing technique are in order.

Getting the colour right

Arriving at the right density for any particular print is very much a matter of judgment, but is not really much more difficult than it is with black and white printing – except that making the tests does of course take longer. But when it comes to getting the colour right, then that is a different matter.

As we have seen earlier in the chapter, when the correct conditions of exposure have been found for one negative on a roll of film, it is usually possible to use the same filtration for the remaining negatives on the roll. The duration of exposure – or the lens aperture will have to be adjusted to allow for any variations in overall density of the negatives, and if the lighting conditions were significantly different for any of the negatives, then this might call for some adjustment in filtration.

Unknown negatives

When you know little or nothing about a colour negative you wish to print, it would be a great help if there were some way in which you could get within striking distance of correct filtration without having to make a lengthy series of preliminary tests.

Integration to grey

This is not the kind of book in which to elaborate on the theoretical principles underlying the mass production of colour snapshots by photofinishing laboratories. However, in so far as the same principles may be used by an amateur when making his own colour prints, then it might pay you to understand something about the concept of integration to grey. In an automatic printer, each negative is analysed by integrating it; so that, in most cases, the machine gets the correct colour and density first time.

It is a somewhat surprising but very useful fact that the overall or integrated colour of the light reflected from a very large number of scenes or subjects is neutral grey. Imagine a scene focused on the ground glass of a camera. If you were to place a diffuser on the lens, to mix up all the light forming the scene, the screen would then be evenly lit overall. With most ordinary scenes it would, in fact, be an even neutral grey. In the same way, the light reflected from a correctly balanced colour print of the scene should also integrate to grey. So, for most scenes a good print on colour paper is produced by adjusting the filtration used so that light emerging from the enlarger lens would, if it were scrambled or diffused, result in a print that looks grey all over.

So, the filter pack needed to print your reference negative is probably

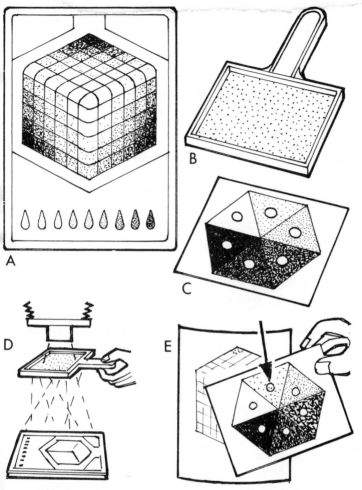

The Unicube mosaic tablet A, comprises a geometric arrangement of three superimposed step wedges made up from the same filters as those supplied by Unicolor for printing. A diffuser – B, is placed beneath the enlarging lens so as to integrate the light from the negative, when a test exposure is made as shown in D. After processing, the test print – E, will usually contain one patch that is neutral grey, to help in deciding just which area is perfectly grey, a perforated mask – C, can be moved across the test print until an exact match is found. The row of "teardrops" at the base of the mosaic is intended to provide an estimate of the exposure that will be required.

the one which produces light that integrates to form a grey image. This means that the amounts of red, green and blue light emerging from the lens (coloured by the negative and the filter) would add up to produce a neutral grey on the paper you are using.

The same proportions of red, green and blue should also produce pretty good prints from a wide variety of other negatives – provided that you continue to use the same batch of paper.

In practice therefore what you aim to do, is to adjust the light transmitted by each new negative so that it would produce a grey colour print if it were integrated before exposing the paper.

Filter mosaics or calculators

That's all very well you may be thinking, but how can I possibly do it? In fact it is quite easy if you use a filter matrix or mosaic – of which there are several kinds available. The Simma Dot Subtractive Calculator, the Mitchell Unicube or the Beseler Calculator are examples.

Each of these calculators, as they are called, comprises an assembly of a range of nearly a hundred different filter combinations in the form of a mosaic tablet. The mosaic is placed in contact with a sheet of colour paper on your enlarger board. You then diffuse the light after it has passed through your negative, filter pack and the enlarger lens. A single exposure yields a print bearing a large number of differently coloured patches – only one of which will be really neutral. Most systems also supply you with a reference to sort out the correct patch. Once you have determined the neutral patch, you simply add the equivalent filters to your pack. Then your whole undiffused print will integrate to grey. If you had a normal negative, and your paper and processing are the same, this should give you a good print.

For the system to work properly, the filters used in making up the mosaic must be the same as those you use in your filter pack. If they are not, then it will usually be necessary to make some allowance for the differences. This simply means that if you plan to use one or other of these calculators then you ought to buy the corresponding set of subtractive printing filters at the same time.

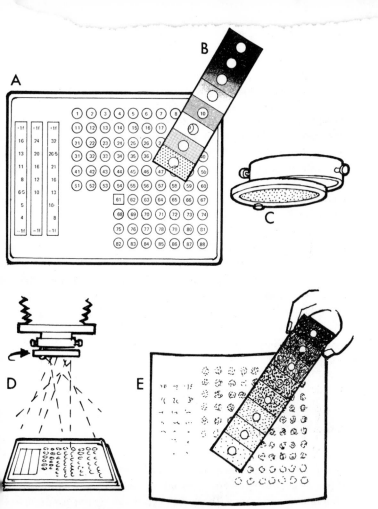

The Simma dot mosaic – A, is laid over a piece of colour paper of the same size and both are located beneath the lens of your enlarger – D. A diffusing disc – C, is attached to the lens and, with a negative in position, a test exposure is made. After processing the print – E, will be covered with a wide range of differently coloured dots – including one that should be neutral grey. It is easier to find the neutral dot if the perforated neutral grey step wedge is used to provide a comparison. The three vertical scales on the mosaic tablet provide information on the test print that will help you to decide the exposure required for each negative.

143

Method not infallible

You should not expect that by using a filter mosaic and following th
simple procedure just outlined, that you will obtain perfect colou
prints from all your negatives at the first time of printing. Integratio
to grey is a kind of averaging method, and while it will work quit
satisfactorily — as it does in photofinishing — for say 90% of the time
there will be some negatives of subjects that had an unusual distribu
tion of colour which could not, by any stretch of imagination be said t
integrate to grey. A close up shot of a bright red car, for example
would integrate to some shade of red and if you made a print of it b
integrating it to grey, any other parts of the picture (a girl's face fo
example) would come out a bluish-green.

Another benefit can be gained from using a filter mosaic or calculato
All of them include a scale of neutrals to provide an indication of th
overall exposure that will be required for any given negative. Her
again the principle of integration is used, simply by assuming that th
integrated density of most average prints is about the same. As an ap
proximation, this is certainly quite useful, and can get your print den
sity about right without too much preliminary testing.

Using an integrating attachment and a calculator, you can thus tes
four separate negatives on one sheet of 8 in × 10 in paper. The result
should let you make a print from each that is adequate in both colou
and density. You may need another print for perfection.

Exposure based on reference negative

You must always remember that the exposing conditions you us
when making your test print in contact with the calculator will b
those which have proved necessary to make a first class print fro
your reference negative. The success you have in using a mosaic filte
calculator depends very much upon the care you took in establishin
optimum filtration and exposure for your standard negative.

Colour analysers

Given that you have found the correct conditions for producing
good print from your standard negative, there is another way in whic

you can use this information to estimate the filtration and exposure required for other negatives.

Instead of using the diffuse light emerging from your enlarger lens to expose a piece of colour paper beneath a filter matrix, you can measure the blue, green and red components of that light by means of a photometer. Then, having changed from your reference negative to a different one, you could, by adjustment of the filter pack or colour head, and the lens aperture, reproduce the values you obtained with the standard negative and then make a print using the new exposing conditions.

In practice, colour analysers or photometers are usually designed to work the other way around. In other words, having set all three channels to zero with the reference negative in the enlarger, the blue, green and red controls on the analyser are then adjusted to regain zero readings when the reference negative is replaced by the un-known one. The resulting settings of the controls then indicate the new filter values.

This description is of course greatly simplified, but since most elec-tronic colour analysers are relatively expensive, not many amateurs are likely to use them, and a more detailed treatment hardly seems necessary. Furthermore, it is generally agreed that there is no form of analyser that will entirely replace judgment – the best that can be expected is some reduction in the number of preliminary tests that have to be made before a perfect print is obtained. So don't feel too badly handicapped if you have to continue to depend upon trial and error. Remember that increasing confidence will come only with experience.

Print viewing conditions

As you become more skilled and more critical of the colour prints you make, you will notice that a print or a test sometimes looks different from one time to another – or even from one room to another. This is because you are examining the print under different kinds of light, so that a result that looked correct last night seems much too blue this morning.

Ideally I suppose, we would like to have daylight available at all times, but even daylight varies considerably according to atmospheric conditions, the time of day and the time of year. So the best compromise is to use what are called colour matching fluorescent lamps. Unfortunately these are not usually stocked by ordinary electrical stores, although they are certainly made by all the main lamp manufacturers. In the U.K., a suitable lamp – Philips 47 – can be obtained from Martin Woolman Ltd., 258 Hatfield Road, St. Albans, Herts.

Colour
Printing
from
Transparencies

In the past, there has been a justifiable belief among photographers that it is much more difficult and usually rather unsatisfactory to make colour prints from transparencies. This belief was not only held by amateurs, but also by photofinishers – whose business it is to make and sell colour prints from both negatives and slides.

One method of getting prints from slides is to make an intermediate colour negative from the original transparency and then to print from the internegative on to colour paper as if it were an original colour negative, but obviously this is a rather expensive and time consuming way of going about the job.

Now things have changed and there are several satisfactory processes available for making colour prints directly from colour transparencies.

Reversal print processes

Broadly, there are now two processes available by which colour prints can be made by direct exposure from a colour transparency. One method uses a three layer print material containing colour couplers, and this is processed by a two-stage reversal procedure involving black and white development followed by colour development.

The other method is to employ a silver dye bleach or dye destruction system whereby dyes that are present in a three layer material when it is coated, are removed during processing to leave the correct amounts of yellow, magenta and cyan to form a composite colour image.

These two different ways of obtaining colour prints from transparencies are described in detail in the next chapter, but the principal difference between the two methods is that a silver-dye-bleach material requires only one development stage and therefore involves a shorter process.

Whichever process you use, there are two very important differences in technique between printing from colour negatives and printing from transparencies. When you make prints from slides you must remember that: 1, more exposure produces a *lighter* print; and 2, a predominant colour cast is corrected by using filters of a complementary colour.

It should help if you have previously made prints only from colour negatives if you study the following table of differences between negative—positive and direct reversal printing.

EFFECTS OF EXPOSURE ON COLOUR REVERSAL PRINTING

If you:	Result by Direct Reversal Printing	Result by Negative–Positive Printing
Increase exposure	Print will be lighter	Print will be darker
Decrease exposure	Print will be darker	Print will be lighter
Double or halve exposure	Significantly lighter or darker print	Significantly darker or lighter print
Print with margins protected during exposure	Borders will be black	Borders will be white
Print from scratched or dusty slides or negatives	Defects will appear black in print	Defects will produce white marks on print
Dodge' or 'hold back' During exposure	Will darken those areas on print	Will lighten those areas
Burn' or 'print-in' during exposure	Will lighten required areas	Will darken areas

Black or white borders

It is interesting that borderless colour prints have recently become extremely popular as a result of the marketing policy adopted by photofinishers in many countries. In fact, it is rather difficult to obtain reversal colour prints with white margins. The reason will be obvious when you think about it – for the margins of the print to be white they must be completely exposed, whereas they are normally protected from exposure by the masking frame of the enlarger easel. The margins of a reversal print will therefore be black, and are probably best trimmed off. If you consider it important to obtain white borders, then you will have to prepare a glass plate with an opaque central area to protect the latent picture image, while you give a flash exposure to thoroughly fog the borders of the print.

EFFECTS OF CHANGES IN FILTRATION
ON COLOUR REVERSAL PRINTING

Required Change	Add – or remove when possible
Less blue (more yellow)	Add yellow or remove magenta and cyan
Less yellow (more blue)	Add magenta and cyan or remove yellow
Less green (more magenta)	Add magenta or remove cyan and yellow
Less magenta (more green)	Add yellow and cyan or remove magenta
Less red (more cyan)	Add cyan or remove yellow and magenta
Less cyan (more red)	Add yellow and magenta or remove cyan

Colour correction and exposure latitude

Although it is not likely that you will often want to print slides that are a long way off colour balance, you will still need a fairly wide range of colour correction filters because larger changes in filter densities are required to bring about a given change in the colour of a print. This advantageous feature of reversal colour printing results from the relatively lower contrast of the print material required when printing from transparencies rather than negatives.

Put another way, reversal colour print materials have a wider latitude in both exposure and filtration than negative printing papers.

Printing speeds

Although they are on the whole slower than colour negative printing papers, all the currently available direct reversal print materials are quite sensitive enough to allow enlargements to be made using normal equipment.

Enlarging equipment

All that has been said in earlier chapters about the various kinds of enlarger and colour heads that are suitable for printing colour negatives applies equally well to an enlarger that will be used to print directly from colour slides.

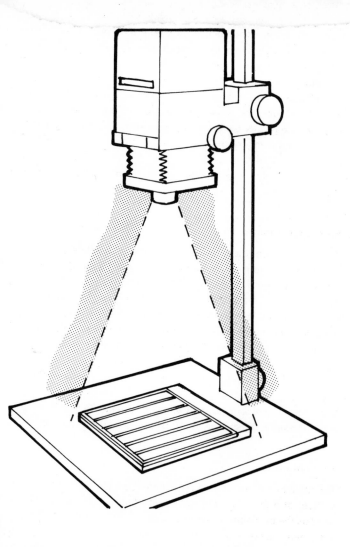

The easiest way to expose a contact print from a set of negatives (or slides) is to use the light from your enlarger. This way, you can easily adjust the filtration and the duration of exposure.

Generally, transparencies can be left in their mounts while they are printed, although if they have been mounted between glass it will be better to remove and remount them in card mounts. This eliminates the four extra surfaces that would almost certainly increase the risks of marks and dust resulting in unnecessary black marks on finished prints. Because the image projected on the base-board of the enlarger is a positive, it is usually quite easy to tell that it is the right way round. To ensure that the image is projected correctly onto the print material, think of your enlarger as a projector and insert each slide accordingly — that is with the emulsion surface away from the enlarging lens.

Reference transparency

Just as it is important to have a reference negative as a yardstick when printing from colour negatives, so it will help you in your early attempts at printing from slides if you choose a well balanced and correctly exposed transparency with which to make your initial tests and subsequent comparisons. When you have arrived at optimum density and colour balance, the exposure conditions generally serve to print other slides of similar density taken on the same brand of film. You will probably find that once you have established the basic filtration it is easier to make colour prints from transparencies than from negatives.

Don't forget to record carefully all the relevant details of the exposure and filtration you used for your best print from your reference slide.

Proof printing

Twenty 2 in × 2 in mounted slides can be proof-printed at one time on a sheet of 8 in × 10 in reversal print material. The enlarger can be used as the exposing source if it is set up so as to enlarge a 24 in × 36 in frame to just over 8 in × 10 in. Assuming that you already know the exposure time required for your reference slide when enlarged to 8 in × 10 in then this same exposure and same filtration should be used to expose your group of slides for proof-printing. The mounted slides can simply be laid on the emulsion surface of a sheet of print material placed in position on the board of the enlarger.

Joining the edges of the slides with strips of adhesive masking tape helps when it comes to positioning them in the dark. The resulting proof sheet will enable you to judge what exposure to give each transparency and whether any of them seem to require colour correction and therefore a different filter pack.

Ring around

As with any other colour printing process, the most difficult thing to learn about direct reversal printing is what direction and degree of exposure and filtration changes are necessary to make a correctly balanced print after having made one that is not quite right. The only way in which a book can help you in this, is to reproduce as accurately as possible a set of ring around prints representing a useful range of differences in filtration. But at best this can only provide a partial solution to the problem – the only really satisfactory way in which you will gain confidence in estimating filter and exposure changes is to make a series of ring around prints for yourself. If you do this, you will soon recover the time you spend and regain more than the value of the print material you use by reducing the number of tests you have to make in future.

Using the reference transparency from which you made the best print you possibly could, make eighteen more prints from this same slide, making the changes in exposure and filtration indicated by the ring around on p. 110.

When you have processed and dried the results, cut them into individual 4 in. × 5 in prints. Mark them with their exposures and filter information before mounting them on a card arranged as shown in the illustration.

Sometimes the difference between the reference print and your test result is greater than any difference illustrated by the prints in your ring around. Then, you will have to use your judgment as to any additional change required. In cases like this, don't be afraid to make substantial adjustments – it is better to go a bit too far and then come back a little than to be not quite sure whether the change was really enough.

Exposure and Processing Reversal Colour Print Materials

Silver-dye-bleach process

Cibachrome is made in Switzerland by the Ilford Group. The Cibachrome process depends on the silver-dye-bleach principle and not on colour development.

Cibachrome has the merit of requiring only three processing steps taking 12 minutes at 24°C. Other advantages claimed for Cibachrome prints are: high colour saturation; excellent sharpness; and great resistance to fading.

The last of these three claims can be made confidently because the azo dyes used in this print material can be chosen — among other properties — for their resistance to fading by light.

In silver-dye bleach or dye-destruction process, the three subtractive dyes — yellow, magenta and cyan — are present in the three emulsion layers at the time of coating, and that proportion of dye that is not required in each layer to form part of the final colour image is destroyed during processing.

Outline of Cibachrome process

When a sheet of Cibachrome print material is exposed to the image of a positive colour transparency — either by contact or in an enlarger, three latent images are formed in the three superimposed emulsion layers in just the same way as with any other colour material. Then, these latent images are developed in a black and white developer to form three *negative* silver images within the yellow, magenta and cyan dyed layers.

These silver images are then bleached away together with the dyes immediately adjacent to them. So the dyes are destroyed selectively in all three layers. Since the silver images were negative, the remaining, unchanged dyes in the three layers are positive images which together form the complete colour picture.

Reversal print materials

If you think about it, you will realise that by using reversal colour processing, it should be possible to obtain a positive colour image by printing from a colour slide on to a sheet of colour paper of the same kind as you would use for printing from a colour negative.

In practice, if you did this, you would get a very contrasty print. The contrast of a colour transparency is much higher than that of a negative. However the idea would have been right, and in fact, apart from their contrast characteristics direct reversal colour development papers are really quite similar to colour negative papers in their construction. The big difference lies in the processing procedure required to produce a positive image from a positive original.

Direct reversal print processing by colour development inevitably involves more processing steps than a negative–positive printing system. The sequence of operations following exposure of a print starts with development of the three negative latent images in a black and white developer. Then, the residual silver halide in all three emulsion layers is fogged either chemically or by exposure to white light. The print is developed again, this time in a colour developer that reacts with the couplers in the emulsions. These produce the required yellow, magenta and cyan positive image components. Of course, at this stage all three layers of the emulsion are totally blackened by the developed silver; the second development having filled in all the gaps in the original negative images. All the silver is removed in a single bleach-fixing treatment, leaving the required composite colour image.

Ektachrome 14 RC

Kodak Pathé in France have worked on reversal colour print processes for many years, and recently they have begun to offer reversal paper and chemicals in kit form for the amateur. Ektachrome 14 RC, as the French product is called, is a resin coated paper that can be processed in about 18 minutes at 30°C.

Ektachrome RC Type 1993

Eastman Kodak in Rochester make another version of a direct reversal colour development material called Ektachrome RC Type 1993, requiring a processing cycle of 21 minutes at 30°C.

During 1976, there were reports that Eastman Kodak were testing a new version of Ektachrome reversal paper – Type 2203. This new

The Cibachrome process

For a long time a major difficulty prevented the wide acceptance of any silver-dye bleach system. Each emulsion layer in effect incorporates a filter dye that is complementary to the sensitivity of the layer. So the printing speed was very low and enlargements – particularly from small negatives – required unacceptably long exposures. This problem has now been overcome, and Cibachrome print material is fast enough for all normal uses. As an example, an 8 in × 10 in enlargement from a 35 mm transparency usually requires an exposure of about 10 seconds at f5.6.

Reciprocity failure

Because there is some slight risk of reciprocity failure if very long exposures are used when printing Cibachrome, it is better to open the aperture of the enlarging lens to keep exposure times as nearly the same as possible.

Safelight

Although a small amount of weak green safelight illumination can be used, it is probably safer and not much more difficult to work in total darkness while exposing Cibachrome print material and loading it into a processing drum.

Identification of emulsion side

Cibachrome print emulsions are coated on a white pigmented acetate sheet which looks rather like a double weight paper and is very smooth on both sides. It is not too easy therefore to be quite sure which side carries the emulsions, but one way of deciding is to lightly pass the tip of your finger over the two surfaces while holding the sheet close to your ear. There will be a slight but distinctive 'whisper' from the *back* side of the material.

ou ever place a sheet of Cibachrome print material in the enlarger
sel the wrong way up, you will quickly realise it once exposure
rts because it will look white, whereas the emulsion surface of the
terial is in fact quite dark because of the dyes incorporated.

arting Filter Pack

e principal reason for using filters when printing from colour slides
to compensate for the characteristic colour balance of the print
terial and the variations between different batches of it. A secon-
ry reason for needing filter adjustment is to compensate for the
aracteristics of your particular enlarging set-up. Thirdly, the filter
ck needs to be changed slightly according to the type of trans-
rency film that you are printing. You must not assume that because
y seem on visual examination to be matched for colour, that an
fachrome slide will print correctly using the same filter pack as the
e you used successfully when printing Kodachromes.

arting filter packs for the more popular makes of transparency film
printed on every packet of Cibachrome print material. For example,
he pack given for Kodachrome is Y70 M00 C25, then this simply
eans that, assuming average enlarging conditions, you should get a
ite well-balanced print from a good Kodachrome slide if you use a
Y together with a 25C filter.

practice you may well find that the suggested starting pack will need
me adjustment to give you the best results under your conditions.

hatever pack you end up by using will probably need to be altered
hen you change to another packet of print material. The alteration
u make will depend simply on the difference between the
commended filters printed on the two packs.

r example:—

ter found best for old batch	Y50 M00 C35
ter recommended on old pack	Y30 M00 C25
fference	Y20 C10
ter recommended on new pack	Y30 M00 C10
ter required with new batch	Y50 M00 C20

Cibachrome P.12 Processing Kits

The Cibachrome processing kit introduced in the U.S. in 1974, is basically the same as the kit sold in Europe since the end of 1975, although the external packaging of the two is quite different – one other difference is that whereas the U.S. kit includes neutralizing tablets for treating used bleach solution before it is discarded, a neutralizing powder is supplied with the kits sold in Europe. The effect of either is the same.

Mixing Cibachrome Developer

The mixing instructions supplied with either of the two Cibachrome P.12 chemical kits are so explicit that it hardly seems necessary to repeat any of the information here. No matter whether you have half a U.S. gallon or two litres of working strength solutions, you are advised to use not less than 90 ml each of developer, bleach and fixer for every 8 in × 10 in print.

Mixed developer will keep for at least four weeks in bottles that are full, and about two weeks if the bottle has air in it.

Mixing Cibachrome Bleach

Cibachrome bleach is different from any other processing solution you are likely to have used in that it is strongly acid and must therefore be handled with care. Ilford advise the use of rubber or plastic gloves while you are preparing the working solutions.

The bleach chemicals are in two parts, 2A in powder form and 2B, a concentrated liquid. The made-up working solution will keep for at least four months.

Fixer

Fixer concentrate is supplied in two bottles in the U.S., while a single, larger bottle is used in Europe. Either is diluted with water to form an equal volume of working strength solution. The working strength solution will keep for at least six months.

Processing Drums

The processing drum sold in the U.S. as part of the Cibachrome A Kit is different from the one supplied by Ilford in Europe. The American drum has a removable cap at each end, so that the central tube can be of different lengths and therefore accommodates different sized prints. The two tube sizes offered with the Cibachrome kit are for 8 in × 10 in and 11 in × 14 in prints.

Another difference lies in the fact that the drum is always placed in a vertical position for the addition of processing solutions or wash water. While vertical, any liquid that is poured into the tank is retained in a reservoir until the drum is moved to a horizontal position, when the solution comes into contact with the print for the first time. This feature is intended to make it easier to achieve accurate processing times. When the required time of treatment has elapsed, the drum is again held in a vertical position, this time over a sink, and then, while the next solution is being poured into the filling end, the used liquid will drain out of the bottom end.

This drum does not have a cam action to provide 'wash-wave' agitation, so it needs an absolutely level bench top. The slightest tilt in the rolling surface will send the liquid to one end of the tube making processing uneven.

The drum that is sold with the Cibachrome kit in European countries is much the same as the Durst Codrum, except that it does not have 'wash-wave' action.

Recommended volumes

The recommended quantity of solution to be used in the 8 in × 10 in Cibachrome drums (see p. 115) is 3 ounces (90 ml) and to use any less solution would be to invite streaking or other kinds of unevenness should the rolling surface not be perfectly level. The quantity of solution recommended for use in the 11 in × 14 in drum is 180 ml (6 ounces). Three well marked plastic measuring beakers are part of the kit, and each of these should be religiously reserved for the same solution in order to avoid contamination.

Processing temperature

Unlike the recommendations given for most colour print processes, Ilford assume that if all your solutions and your tank are allowed to assume the ambient temperature of the room in which you are working, say between 68°F and 82°F (20°C to 28°C) – then you will merely need to adjust treatment times appropriately in order to achieve standardised results. The temperature latitude of this process is one of its advantages, especially for the amateur.

The times for each step at 68°F, 75°F and 82°F are given below:

PROCESSING TIMES FOR CIBACHROME

	68°F ± 3°F (20°C ± 1 °C)	75°F ± 3°F (24°C ± 1 °C)	82°F ± 3°F (29°C ± 1 °C)
Development	2½ minutes	2 minutes	1½ minutes
Bleaching	4½ minutes	4 minutes	3½ minutes
Fixing	3½ minutes	3 minutes	2½ minutes
Washing	3½ minutes	3 minutes	2½ minutes
Total time	14 minutes	12 minutes	10 minutes

Control of contrast

Some control over contrast can be obtained by adjusting the time in the black and white developer within, say, plus or minus half a minute. Extend development time to obtain slightly higher contrast and reduce it for softer results.

Rinse after development

Although it is not strictly necessary, it is advisable to use a short rinse between development and bleaching. This removes any residual

162

developer and so avoids any unpleasant smell when the strongly acid bleach solution is poured into the drum.

Bleaching

Do not reduce the time allowed for bleaching or let up on the agitation during the bleaching stage. As the bleaching reaction goes to completion you can do no harm by over-bleaching.

Neutralizing bleach solution

Because it is strongly acid you should collect used bleach solution with all the other solutions in a plastic bucket. At the end of your processing session add the neutralizing tablets or powder (provided in your kit) before pouring the accumulated waste solution down the drain. Instead of the tablets or powder you can use bicarbonate of soda – one tablespoon to each 100 ml of used bleach.

Fixing

A three minute fixing step follows bleaching and since this reaction also goes to completion, it should not normally introduce any kind of variation in your finished results.

Washing

After fixing, the print must be washed free of chemicals before being dried. The washing can either take place in the tank or, if you have already removed the print to see what it is like, you can wash it in a dish. In either case, three minutes in running water will be enough. While it is often very tempting to judge the quality of a Cibachrome print immediately after fixing and before washing, you should realise that while it is wet a Cibachrome print looks slightly more magenta than it will after it has been dried.

Ektachrome 14 RC Paper

This resin coated paper is the fastest of all the currently available direct reversal colour print materials and of course is sensitive to light of all colours. Kodak Pathé, the manufacturer, gives no recommendations for safelighting, but sensibly advise you to work in total darkness.

Storage

As with most other colour materials, it is best to store Ektachrome 14 RC paper at a low temperature – say at 10°C or less. However, a week or so at room temperature (20° – 25°C) is unlikely to cause any discernible change in the performance of the paper.

U.V. Filters

Ektachrome RC paper should be protected from any ultra-violet light that might pass through both the transparency and enlarger lens. A Kodak CP2B filter or its equivalent should therefore be permanently housed in the filter drawer.
A heat absorbing glass is also necessary to protect both filters and the slides you will be printing.

Importance of heat absorber

Your slides are usually left in their mounts while you are printing from them so there is always a risk that the film will 'pop' in the same way as it sometimes does in a slide projector. This makes the use of a heat absorbing filter very important. It reduces the risk of popping.

Exposure times

It is quite impossible to predict exactly the exposure you will need when making an enlargement from a side; however, some kind of guide is better than nothing when you are about to make your very first tests. Supposing you are enlarging a 24 × 36 mm transparency on to an 8 in × 10 in sheet, you will probably be somewhere near right with one or other of your tests if you make an exposure series giving 2, 4, 8 and 16 seconds at *f*.8.

Filter values

Each packet of Ektachrome 14 RC paper bears a set of filter ratings and an exposure rating that are characteristic of that particular batch of paper. As with any other colour printing process, whenever you have to change from one batch of paper to another, you will need to do a little arithmetic in order to calculate – as nearly as possible – the new combination of filters to use.

Suppose for example you have found that to get a balanced print from your reference transparency you were using a 20 Y and 35 C pack, and the filter rating given on the old package of paper was 10 Y and 30 C. Then the difference between the two would be 10 Y and 5 C, and these values should then be added to the filter ratings given on the new packet of paper. Say these new values are 20 Y and 20 C, then the filter pack to try would be 30 Y and 25 C.

If you were using lower densities in your old filter pack than those indicated on the package of your previous batch of paper, then the differences between the two will be minus in value and they should be subtracted from the filter ratings printed on your new packet. For example, the pack you were using successfully comprised 20 Y and 35 C, and the rating for the batch of paper was 30 Y and 40 C. The difference is 10 Y and 5 C. If the values given for your new batch of paper are 20 Y and 20 C, you should start testing with a pack comprising 10 Y and 15 C.

Exposure rating

The exposure coefficient given on each packet of Ektachrome 14 RC is simply a factor (based on 100) which can be used to relate the exposures you found to be correct with one batch of paper with the exposures you will need – with the same or equivalent transparencies – when you come to use the new batch of paper.

To take a simple example, if the exposure time for your reference transparency was 10 seconds on the old batch of paper and it had an exposure rating of 100, then the next batch, supposing it has an exposure rating of 120, will need 12 seconds exposure (i.e. 10 × 120/100).

Ektaprint R 14 liquid chemistry

Ektaprint R 14 chemistry is supplied in kit form to make 1 litre each of five working strength solutions. These five working baths are made up from nine bottles, grouped as follows:

First Developer	2 bottles (A and B)
Stop Bath	1 bottle
Colour Developer	3 bottles (A, B and C)
Bleach-fix	2 bottles (A and B)
Stabiliser	1 bottle

Mixing instructions

Among the instructions included with Ektaprint R 14 chemistry, there are one or two points worth repeating:

1 At least three mixing vessels should be used to avoid contamination. Use them exclusively for the first developer and stop bath, the colour developer, and the bleach-fix and stabiliser.
2 Always rinse out the concentrate bottles with a little water that is then added to the solution you are making up.
3 Do not divide the concentrates in an attempt to make up smaller quantities of working solution than those specified. (No explanation is given for this advice.)
4 Do not mix air into the solutions when you stir them. Excessive stirring serves no purpose – two minutes should be sufficient.

Keeping qualities

Kodak stress the importance of storing the working solutions for the Ektaprint R 14 process in tightly stoppered *full* bottles. In practice, this advice is somewhat difficult to follow. One partial solution to this problem is to store the made up solutions in several smaller bottles – which can be plastic – thereby ensuring that some of your working solution remains in sealed containers until you need it. As an alternative, you can top up nearly full bottles with inert solids, such as glass marbles. Also, there are now available concertina bottles. You simply press on the top of the bottle until it squashes down to the level of the liquid. Screw on the stopper and you have expended all the air.

In stoppered bottles, stored at reasonably low temperatures (less than 10°C (50°F)) the keeping periods will be at least 2 weeks for the two developers, 3 weeks for the bleach-fix and 8 weeks for the stop bath and stabiliser.

Processing

When using the Kodak Printank – or equivalent 8 in × 10 in processing drum – it is recommended that 60 ml of each solution should be used.

Contamination

As with any other process, care must be taken to avoid contamination of one solution by another. Reversal colour development processes require rather more care because they involve the use of more solutions.

If at any time you find that your prints persistently lack density and have either a blue or cyan cast, then that is the time to carefully check your routine in case you are unwittingly allowing contamination to creep in at some stage of the process.

Processing procedure

The instructions packed with Ektaprint R 14 chemistry assume that you will be using a Kodak Printank and that you will control the temperature of each processing solution by floating and rotating the tank on the surface of a water bath maintained at one degree centigrade higher than the stipulated processing temperature (i.e. 31°C). If on the other hand you plan to use a Simmard or similar processor, you can use a nomograph or scale to find what the temperature of your pre-heat water should be to suit the ambient room temperature and provide the necessary solution temperature inside the tank — which in this case is 30°C.

THE PROCESSING STEPS FOR EKTAPRINT R 14

Step	Time
Pre-wet*	30 seconds
First development	3 minutes
Stop	1–30 seconds
Wash	2 minutes
Reversal Exposure †	15 seconds
Colour Development	3 minutes 30 seconds
Wash	2 minutes
Bleach-fix	3 minutes
Wash	3 minutes
Stabilise	1 minute

* Note that even if you are using a Printank, or any other method which does not use a presoak bath for temperature control, a pre-wet is still necessary. Pour 500 ml of water into the tank and agitate 30 seconds before pouring away.

† To give this reversal exposure, remove the print from the tank at the end of the 2 minutes washing step and expose it for at least 15 seconds to a 60 watt lamp at a distance of 18 inches (0.5 metre).

Ektachrome RC Paper Type 1993

This reversal colour paper is made by Eastman Kodak in the U.S. and it differs in several significant ways from Ektachrome 14 RC.

Reversal exposure or chemical fogging

Reversal colour print processes often require re-exposure of the unused parts of the emulsion layers prior to colour development of the three component colour positive images. It is possible to dispense with reversal exposure by incorporating a chemical fogging agent in the colour developer itself. The Ektaprint 14 process used for Kodak Pathe's Ektachrome 14 RC paper does require re-exposure, but the Ektaprint RD process for Eastman Kodak's Type 1993 reversal colour print paper uses a colour developer with a fogging agent.

Printing speed

The 14 RC material made in France is much faster than the Type 1993 paper made in Rochester by Eastman Kodak. The American material is slower than any of the Ektacolor papers intended for printing from colour negatives, so that even a 8 in × 10 in enlargement from a 35 mm slide may require an exposure of 30 seconds at $f4.5$ with a typical enlarger.

Special printing filters

In order to minimise the differences in printing characteristics between Ektachrome and Kodachrome transparencies, Eastman Kodak recommends the use of a special dichroic filter – No. 301 – in the printing beam. This advice is really intended for the large scale user who wants to print a mixture of Kodachrome and Ektachrome slides, without making any adjustment to the filter pack. The amateur can dispense with the 301 filter if he will make any necessary filter adjustments whenever he prints from different kinds of slide film.

Processing Type 1993 colour paper

One way of reducing the otherwise long processing cycle with a reversal colour paper is to use wash water at a fairly high temperature and to use changes of water rather than large volumes or a rapid flow. By washing with water at about 38°C (100°F), it is possible to reduce the overall wet processing time for a Type 1993 print to around 17 minutes without having to use excessively high developer temperatures.

ONE EKTAPRINT RD PROCEDURE

Step	Time	Temperature
Pre Soak	1 minute	38°C (100°F)
First Developer	2 minutes	24°C (75°F)
Stop	30 seconds	24°C (75°CF)
Wash	5 × 15 seconds	38°C (100°F)
Colour Developer	4 minutes	24°C (75°F)
Wash	2 × 15 seconds	38°C (100°F)
Bleach-fix	2 minutes	24°C (75°F)
Wash	8 × 15 seconds	38°C (100°F)
Stabiliser	2 minutes	24°C (75°F)
Wash	2 × 15 seconds	38°C (100°F)

Opalescence of wet prints

Because it uses the same kind of couplers as all the other Kodak colour papers, a wet Ektachrome print has a pronounced bluish opalescent appearance and its colour cannot be reliably assessed until it has been dried.

Drying prints

You can dry your Ektachrome RC prints with a fan heater or a hair dryer, or you can simply hang them from a line or lay them out on blotting paper or muslin covered racks.
Don't try to glaze them on a flat-bed or a rotary glazer.

Modifying and
Finishing
Colour Prints

Local density control during printing

When the sky area of a black and white print looks too light and devoid of the clouds that can be seen in the negative, it is a comparatively simple job to make another print and give the sky additional exposure by burning in. When the area to be modified is large and well defined, the extra exposure can be given simply by using the hand to prevent any additional light from reaching the foreground of the picture. More complicated areas can be burned in by means of suitably shaped holes cut in stiff black paper. Of course, whatever is used as the mask, it must be held fairly well away from the paper plane and kept gently moving so as to avoid a hard line of demarcation.

Dodging

Dodging or holding back is the opposite of burning in. It too can be done with the hand or with suitably shaped pieces of black paper attached to the end of wires – devices sometimes known as paddles. Exactly the same methods can be used when colour printing with the white-light or subtractive method. In fact these techniques can be developed still further when colour as well as density needs to be changed.

Modifying density and colour

Instead of simply darkening the sky area of a print by additional local exposure, you can make it a stronger blue by making the extra exposure through a yellow or orange filter. In the same way when printing from a colour negative it is sometimes possible to make the sea in a seascape look bluer by giving additional local exposure through a red filter.

Correcting prints from transparencies

The techniques of colour correction during printing are probably easier to learn when printing from transparencies, since then the effects of any local filtration will be much easier to understand and see. But remember that because of the relatively low contrast of reversal print materials, stronger filters will be required to produce a given alteration than you would need when printing from a colour negative.

One important point to remember is that you are *reducing* the light with your dodging. So if you want to change the colour without altering the density, you must give some of the exposure through the filter as an extra, while the rest of the print is covered.

Retouching colour negatives or transparencies

While it is possible for a skilled retoucher to make corrections or alterations directly on a colour negative, it is certainly beyond the ability of most amateurs. In the same way, although colour transparencies can be (and often are) retouched and modified for reproduction purposes, the job is beyond the skill of most of us.

There is one kind of correction that should be made on the negative and that is the blotting out of any pin holes or scratches that would result in totally black blemishes in any print that is made. Since it is much more difficult to remove a black spot from a print than it is to fill in a white spot, small 'minus density' defects on a negative should be neatly covered with an opaque paint of some kind using a No. 1 sable brush. They then make corresponding white areas on the print.

Handwork on prints

Because the size is larger and visual effects are more easily seen, most of us will resort to working directly on our print if we need to change the straightforward processed result. Bearing in mind that skilled colour print finishers are rather rare and very highly paid, we should not be too ambitious in our early attempts at correcting prints by hand. Practice alone will lead to the skill required to modify areas of a colour print without obvious evidence of the work that has been done.

To start with you will probably limit your efforts to spotting out the blemishes that result from dust or scratches. Lots of patience, a set of three subtractive coloured (cyan, magenta and yellow) dyes or water colours, and a good quality (No. 1 or 2) sable brush are all that you need for this job.

Several photographic companies sell sets of retouching dyes and often the colours have been chosen to match the subtractive dyes formed in their particular colour print material. So whenever possible, use dyes that are offered by whoever makes your colour paper. But if you find these special dyes difficult to obtain or more expensive than you feel is justified for the small amount of use you have for them, then you can try using water colours. Although slightly more opaque than dyes, most water colours are sufficiently transparent not to be noticed on the surface of a finished print – particularly if a little gum is used with the colour. If you buy these colours in pans you will find them more useful than in tubes.

When deciding how much of each colour you need to apply to match a blemish into its surrounding area remember that the image you are working on results from varying proportions of yellow, magenta and cyan dyes and you should therefore be able to obtain an almost perfect match by applying one or more of your three spotting colours in the right amounts and proportions.

I find that spotting with a brush is easier to do when the emulsion surface of the print is slightly damp. This is a little more difficult with Kodak papers because of the opalescent appearance that persists until the print is dry. But whether you work on a moist or dry print, you will find that a stippling technique with a semi-dry brush will give you the greatest control. After picking up the dye or water colour on your brush, remove all surplus on a sheet of blotting paper, leaving the brush just moist enough to transfer controllable amounts of colour to the surface of the print.

For much simpler spotting, you may find that you can get away with using a single dark grey or brown colour. When you have only tiny areas to cover, you don't really need to get them the right colour. If they are *exactly* the right density, for normal viewing your eyes will automatically colour them to match the surroundings. Naturally, neutral coloured spots will not go undiscovered in a minute examination; so colours are needed for perfection as they are for retouching for larger areas.

Removing colours

Now that colour print materials are almost all made on resin coated base, areas cannot easily be removed by knifing because there is a tendency for the polyethylene layer to pick up and permanently spoil the surface of the print. The only way round this difficulty is to remove the blemishes by chemical bleaching, before spotting back to match the surrounding area.

Bleaching procedure

Three stock solutions should be prepared for bleaching out black spots on colour prints:

1 Potassium permanganate
   Water to   500 ml

2 Sulphuric acid (conc.)   50 ml
   Added to   450 ml of water.

   Always add the acid to the water and stir while doing so.

3 Sodium metabisulphite   10 grams
   Water to   500 ml

For use, mix equal parts of 1 and 2 – say 25 ml of each, and procede to spot out blemishes. Bleaching may take 2 minutes or so, but when it is complete, cover the areas you have treated with the solution of metabisulphite and leave for about half a minute until the brown stain disappears.
Finally, wash the whole print for 2 or 3 minutes and re-stabilise, if a stabilising step was included in the processing cycle.
In the case of large or very dense blemishes, bleaching and cleaning can be repeated several times with merely a rinse between treatments.

Mounting colour prints

No matter whether your print is on a resin coated paper base or on a white pigmented acetate base such as is used for Cibachrome, you will not be able to use any of the old simple methods of mounting with water based paste. The reason is simply that there is no way in which the paste can dry out by evaporation through the print. There is no problem if you are using a porous mount through which it can dry. For most purposes, however, it is best to use a double faced adhesive sheet such as is made by Adpak or Lomacoll. If you cannot obtain sheets of double faced adhesive material, then narrow double sided adhesive tape can be applied to the back of your print in a criss cross pattern.

Colour prints can be dry-mounted – either in a press or by using a domestic hand iron. Dry mounting tissues now work at lower temperatures than were once required. Even so a test should be made, using a waste print, before any important photograph is mounted. The surface of the print – particularly if it is glossy – should be protected with a sheet of silicon release paper – obtainable from the suppliers of dry mounting tissue. On no account should the temperature be allowed to exceed 93°C. If it does, the resin coating may start to melt. You can buy temperature-sensitive wax cones so that you can set the precise temperature on your equipment. Once you have determined a maximum setting, *never* go beyond it.

Permanence of prints on display

In the earlier days of colour printing, the permanence of the dyes used to form an image were greatly suspect. Most of us remember seeing badly faded colour prints in house agents windows, but nowadays colour print materials are all greatly improved in this respect. While no manufacturer would go so far as to claim that the dyes used in his colour paper will never fade or change in any way, you can rest assured that unless you place your prints in direct sunlight, you are unlikely to detect any significant change in them for a long time.

This is one feature which is particularly attributable to dye-destruction prints. Such prints, although not eternal, do have a longer life in sunlight than prints produced in a colour development process.

Black and white prints from colour negatives

Because of the coloured masking densities that are present in all modern colour negatives, it is quite difficult to get any kind of black and white print from such negatives on normal — blue sensitive — bromide paper. Yet there are occasions when it is very useful to be able to make a quick black and white proof of a colour shot, or to be able to make a number of black and white prints when it would be too expensive or take too long to make that number of prints in colour. With these considerations in mind, Kodak produce their Panalure monochrome printing paper — a panchromatic material that is processed in just the same way as any other black and white enlarging paper. However, it must be handled in complete darkness, or under a colour processing safelight, such as Kodak 10 H filtered 25 watt lamp.

Because you are likely to be dish developing this paper (in your normal black-and-white solutions), even this dim safelight is a considerable help. It is, however, much too dark for any inspection, so you must develop by the recommended time and temperature method. To see slightly better, you may find one of the pulsating 'colour' safelights a useful addition to your darkroom.

As it is panchromatic, the tone reproduction obtainable with Panalure is comparable with that obtained with panchromatic film when photographing a normal portrait or scene. In other words hair, eyes and lips in a portrait picture printed on Panalure will appear as correct relative densities, while clouds in a blue sky will be well recorded instead of disappearing as they would if ordinary bromide paper were to be used.

Index